AMUSING THE MILLION

*Coney Island at the
Turn of the Century*

JOHN F. KASSON

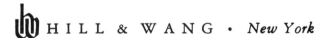 HILL & WANG · *New York*

Also by John F. Kasson
CIVILIZING THE MACHINE
RUDENESS AND CIVILITY

Hill and Wang
A division of Farrar, Straus and Giroux
19 Union Square West, New York 10003

Library of Congress Cataloging-in-Publication Data
Kasson, John F. Amusing the million.
(American century series)
Bibliography: p.   Includes index.
1. Coney Island, N.Y. 2. New York (City)
—Social life and customs. I. Title.
F129.C75K37   1978   301.29'747'23   78-6762

Paperback ISBN: 0-8090-0133-0

Designed by Jacqueline Schuman

www.fsgbooks.com

25   27   29   31   32   30   28   26   24

For Joy
who helped immeasurably in the writing

and for Peter
who can look at the pictures

ACKNOWLEDGMENTS

I am grateful to a number of people for aid in the writing of this book. Craig Stewart helped stimulate the idea behind it. Carl and Jane Smith, Richard Blau, Henry Binford, Stephen Marini, and Peter Filene offered vital encouragement on an early draft. The members of the Social History Workshop made an invaluable contribution with supportive criticism and hard questions, which Joseph Tulchin thoughtfully summarized; I hope that I have answered some of them. Arthur W. Wang's enthusiasm heartened me throughout the project. David Schuyler gave indispensable aid in several errands of research. A large number of people and institutions helped in gathering the illustrations. Let me here thank especially Marie Spina of the Brooklyn Public Library, Steven Miller and Esther Brumberg of the Museum of the City of New York, Jerry L. Kearns of the Library of Congress, Elaine Bak of the Long Island Historical Society, Jane Hoffer, and Mr. and Mrs. Albert H. Gordon. Rosalie Radcliffe typed the manuscript with dispatch and unfailing good humor. My largest debt in this endeavor as in so many others is to my wife, Joy S. Kasson.

Coney Island: the name still resonates with a sense of excitement, the echo of an earlier age. Once commanding two miles of beach on the southwestern end of Long Island, the amusement center has seen its domain dwindle to an area sixteen blocks long and two wide. Coney now lives largely on the borrowed capital of its past. It wears an air of faded glory, making it a favorite subject of Sunday-supplement articles and anecdotal tributes. But despite the nostalgia Coney Island arouses, the historical context in which it established its enduring national reputation remains neglected. As a result, Coney's true significance has scarcely been grasped. The era of Coney Island's famous amusement parks began in 1895, and they flourished in the years before the First World War. Coney's heyday thus coincided with a critical period in American history, when the nation came of age as an urban-industrial society and its citizens eagerly but painfully adjusted to the new terms of American life. Changing economic and social conditions helped to create the basis of a new mass culture which would gradually emerge in the first decades of the twentieth century. At the turn of the century this culture was still in the process of formation and not fully incorporated into the life of society as a whole. Its purest expression at this time lay in the realm of commercial amusements, which were creating symbols of the new cultural order, helping to knit a heterogeneous audience into a cohesive whole. Nowhere were these symbols and their relationship to the new mass audience more clearly revealed than at turn-of-the-century Coney Island.

So major was the cultural upheaval Coney Island dramatized that it is difficult to recapture the age that went before it. Nineteenth-century America was governed by a strikingly coherent set of values, a culture in many respects more thoroughly "Victorian" than the England over which Victoria reigned. Beginning in the antebellum period, a self-conscious elite of critics, ministers, educators, and reformers, drawn principally from the Protestant middle class of the urban Northeast, had arisen to assume cultural leadership. In the wake of the disintegration of the old colonial gentry class, these genteel reformers took as their mission to discipline, refine, and instruct the turbulent urban-industrial democracy. American apostles of culture strenuously labored to inculcate the Victorian virtues of "character"—moral integrity, self-control, sober earnestness, industriousness—among the citizenry at large. Ideally, they believed, all activities both in work and in leisure should be ultimately constructive. Hard work improved the individual as well as society, curbing men's animal passions, which if unchecked would bring about social collapse. Leisure, too, should be spent not in idleness but in edifying activities. Under their auspices, poetry, fiction, the visual arts, and related pursuits were legitimized not "for art's sake" but for their moral and social utility.[1]

Throughout most of the nineteenth century this genteel culture occupied a position as the "official" culture which deviant individuals and groups might defy but not as yet displace. Genteel reformers founded museums, art galleries, libraries, symphonies, and other institutions which set the terms of formal cultural life and established the cultural tone that dominated public discussion. Of critical importance to their success as cultural arbiters was their ability to enlist the support of influential shapers of the nascent mass culture, who echoed their tone and carried their message to a broad audience. This alliance between "high" and "middle" culture, between members of the cultural elite and commercial tastemakers, made the hegemony of the genteel culture possible. A series of technological innovations permitted widespread dissemination of inexpensive books, periodicals, engravings, lithographs, photographs, and other mass reproductions—the beginnings of the communications revolution which has so characterized our own time. As nineteenth-century cultural entrepreneurs sought to develop a vast new market, they popularized genteel values and conceptions of art. The editors of the leading popular magazines and monthlies, the new mass publishers, the most widely respected writers, lecturers, and artists participated in the commercialization of American culture; but in their public postures they resolutely directed their gazes above the coarse and vulgar realities of everyday life to the lofty realm of the ideal. In a mobile, culturally insecure nation, acquisition of reproduced objets d'art, familiarity with "uplifting" writers, and espousal of genteel values became badges of status and refinement.

Despite its considerable following, however, this genteel or "Victorian" culture by no means penetrated all aspects of American life. The United States in the nineteenth century contained a strikingly heterogeneous and diverse population with a variety of cultures and subcultures. Genteel cultural reformers never achieved the control they sought, a fact they readily acknowledged. To reconcile social change with order, industrial growth with stability, democracy with authority, was the extraordinary challenge they set themselves. From their perspective whatever gains they achieved appeared modest in the face of the immense problems that remained. Despite determined efforts, they particularly sensed their failure to exert a pervasive influence upon the urban working classes and new immigrant groups, both of whom clung as best they could to their own cultural forms and values. In the later nineteenth century, moreover, an assertive new economic elite arose with less intimate ties to the custodians of culture. While some genteel reformers successfully formed alliances with these figures, often they found their social position overshadowed by the nouveaux riches, their authority in eclipse. Resentfully, genteel spokesmen castigated the great industrialists as cultural barbarians, without education, refinement, responsibility, or restraint. By the end of the nineteenth century at both ends of the social scale, middle-class cultural arbiters felt the limits of their power.

Still more distressing, they soon discovered a rebellion among their very own children as well. A distinctly new generation came of age around the turn of the century, impatient with the intellectual and emotional restraints, stifled by the insulating comforts of genteel middle-class existence. Many of this generation's leading minds hungered to immerse themselves in issues and experience outside the categories of genteel respectability—in the lives of the urban working class and ethnic minorities, in muckraking journalism of business and politics, in artistic realism and modernism, in feminism, education, and other fields. The limitations of genteel culture as an approach to a sprawling urban-industrial democracy appeared exposed as never before.[2]

Slowly at first in the late nineteenth century, then quickly as the twentieth century advanced, the genteel middle-class cultural order crumbled. And the entrepreneurs of mass culture, who had previously helped solidify the authority of genteel values, discovered new opportunities outside its confines. Hitherto, relatively few major commercial entertainers openly ventured beyond the pale of middle-class respectability. Popular impresarios such as P. T. Barnum learned to master the rhetoric of moral elevation, scientific instruction, and cultural refinement in presenting their attractions—from the Feejee Mermaid to the Swedish Nightingale, Jenny Lind. But by the turn of the century the managers of mass culture sensed new markets both within the urban middle class and spilling beyond its borders to "high society" and the largely untapped working class, all eager to respond to amusement in a less earnest cultural mood: more vigorous, exuberant, daring, sensual, uninhibited, and irreverent. As a result, American mass culture embraced activities which had previously existed only on the margins of American life.

Examples of this transformation abound. Beginning with ragtime and the cakewalk in the 1890s, Afro-American music and dance

emerged out of black communities and the demimonde to be commercialized and transformed for white urban audiences. Vigorous,
violent sports such as prizefighting, earlier confined to gentlemen's
clubs or working-class saloons, gained increased popular acceptance;
and competitive athletics in general attracted large new followings
both on college campuses and on professional playing fields. At the
turn of the century a new wave of popular literature broke with the
genteel code of delicacy, domesticity, and decorum, in such celebrations of masculine toughness and violence as Owen Wister's *The
Virginian* (1902), Jack London's *The Call of the Wild* (1903), and
Edgar Rice Burroughs's *Tarzan of the Apes* (1914). And the movies
in the space of a few years moved from penny arcades, billiard
parlors, and crude storefront "nickelodeons" in working-class and
immigrant neighborhoods to captivate an immense audience by the
time of the First World War.[3]

The most striking expression of the changing character of American culture, however, lies in the new amusement parks that were
developed at the turn of the century. Made possible by swelling
urban populations and an increase in leisure time and spending power
and spurred by the development of electric trolley systems that
allowed inexpensive excursions from the city, amusement parks
rapidly proliferated throughout the country. Boston's Paragon Park
and Revere Beach, Philadelphia's Willow Grove and nearby Atlantic
City, Atlanta's Ponce de Leon Park, Cleveland's Euclid Beach,
Chicago's Cheltenham Beach, Riverview, and White City, St. Louis's
Forest Park Highlands, Denver's Manhattan Beach, San Francisco's
The Chutes—these and others large and small became meccas for a
public eagerly seeking recreation. Dominating them all in size, scope,
and fame was New York's Coney Island.

Amusement parks at Coney Island and elsewhere gathered
together a variety of popular attractions and pastimes, all of which
reflected the changing cultural mood. These might include bathing
facilities, band pavilions, dance halls, vaudeville theaters, and circus
attractions. The amassing of these varied entertainments, however,
was not what made the parks most remarkable. Their special distinc-

tion lay in the new mechanical amusements and exotic settings they provided and the response these sparked among huge crowds of pleasure seekers. In most entertainments of the period the public remained in the position of spectators—at baseball, football, and boxing contests, at vaudeville, variety, and movie theaters. At Coney Island and other amusement parks, by contrast, audience and activity frequently merged. Drawing upon a broad, heterogeneous urban public, amusement parks stirred them into activity. Customers participated intimately in the spectacle about them. The relationship between entertainment and the cultural needs of the audience was far more striking than in spectator pastimes. Amusement parks emerged as laboratories of the new mass culture, providing settings and attractions that immediately affected behavior. Their creators and managers pioneered a new cultural institution that challenged prevailing notions of public conduct and social order, of wholesome amusement, of democratic art—of all the institutions and values of the genteel culture. Amusement complexes such as Coney Island thus shed light on the cultural transition and the struggle for moral, social, and aesthetic authority that occurred in the United States at the turn of the century.

Previous accounts of Coney Island have failed to grasp its larger significance. Much of the writing has been in the vein of "The Night They Burned the Old Nostalgia Down," elegiac accounts that concentrate on Coney Island's internal history and treat it as a curiosity, an independent principality of play. But considered from a broader cultural perspective, Coney's features take on new importance. As one looks closely at turn-of-the-century photographs, they shed their quaint aspect to disclose the meaning they held for participants. When read carefully, old magazine accounts of visits to the Island raise far more serious issues than one would at first suppose from their often jocular tone. Explored afresh in this way, Coney Island no longer appears an object of nostalgia; rather it emerges as a harbinger of modernity. The popular resort quickly became a symbol not only of fun and frolic but also of major changes in American manners and morals.

Coney thus offers a case study of the growing cultural revolt against genteel standards of taste and conduct that would swell to a climax in the 1920s. The new amusement parks and their patrons attracted the attention of a variety of critics, artists, and reformers. In studying Coney Island these observers felt themselves confronting in intensified form the face of a new mass culture. They pondered the complexion of this emergent culture and wondered what rules and restraints would replace those which were being swept away. Coney Island ultimately precipitated a debate that has continued up to our own time over the role and significance of popular amusement in a democracy. The story of the resort illuminates the character of the mass culture that would soon dominate American life.

The challenge of Coney Island and the new mass culture it represented emerges most clearly when contrasted with two highly influential earlier models of urban recreation developed by genteel reformers in the second half of the nineteenth century, New York's Central Park and Chicago's Columbian Exposition of 1893. Despite important differences in philosophy and form, the two projects represented a broad common effort: to provide cultural leadership for an urban-industrial society; to present a model of social order, cohesion, and tranquillity for a fractious people; to elevate public taste and reform public conduct. Both enterprises were designed not simply to amuse but to instruct their users in lessons of aesthetic taste and social responsibility and to inspire them with a respect for cultural standards.

Though this reformist vision was shared by a number of influential figures, its preeminent apostle was the great environmental designer Frederick Law Olmsted. Born into a rural republic in 1822, Olmsted made the central concern of his career how to retain proximity with nature in what was swiftly becoming a nation of cities. While he celebrated the city as the proper and inevitable center of

Frederick Law Olmsted

modern civilization, he decried the reckless and haphazard course of urban growth in the nineteenth century, guided almost exclusively by narrow commercial interests. He measured the cost not only in the most obvious "social failures": the swelling ranks of criminals and prostitutes, of the alcoholic, insane, diseased, and the poor. For Olmsted the effects of the relentless commercial environment so pervaded the culture of cities that they might be observed simply by walking through a business district. There the crowded sidewalks demanded that pedestrians make the constant mental effort of observing and anticipating the movements of passersby, merely to avoid collision. Urban dwellers wore the mark of such habitual calculations, Olmsted noted. Along with "a remarkable quickness of apprehension," they displayed "a peculiarly hard sort of selfishness. Every day of their lives they have seen thousands of their fellow-men, have met them face to face, have brushed against them, and yet have had no experience of anything in common with them." Contact without fellowship, congregation without community—these were characteristics of urban mass society that troubled Olmsted and other genteel reformers, including the poet and journalist William Cullen Bryant, the landscape architect Andrew Jackson Downing, the influential Unitarian minister Henry Whitney Bellows, and the urban social worker Charles Loring Brace. They advocated large public parks as necessary institutions of democratic recreation and indispensable antidotes to urban anomie.[4]

Town commons and greens had existed in America since the seventeenth century, of course, but the public park, specifically designed for recreation, remained an innovation of the nineteenth, a direct response to the new industrial city. The first major public park in the United States was New York's Central Park, which was designed by Olmsted in collaboration with Calvert Vaux in 1858. In it Olmsted attempted to embody his conception of democratic recreation.

Olmsted intended the park to serve, above all, as a rural retreat in the midst of the city, an easily accessible refuge from urban pressures and conditions. City dwellers would shed the fatigue and

Crowds on Broadway, 1875

monotony of New York's grid of streets as they explored the park's artfully natural landscape. Its meandering paths led visitors on a continuing series of discoveries: by pastoral meadows and picturesque woods, rolling hills and soothing lakes. The primary recreational value of the park, Olmsted insisted, consisted in this contemplation of natural scenery. The park also provided limited opportunities for other activities: horseback riding, summer boating and winter skating, and various amusements for children. However, Olmsted made little provision for the desire of working-class males to have "manly and blood-tingling recreations," "boisterous fun and rough sports." The planners steadfastly resisted any installations or practices that threatened to compromise the scenic integrity of the park as a whole. In this way, Olmsted hoped, the park would offer both physical and imaginative exercise and create a setting where people of all classes might promenade in large groups or picnic in small ones.

13

Central Park, 1863

Thus Olmsted firmly believed that the aesthetic experience of the park would pay social and moral dividends. It would soothe discontent and encourage sociability through restorative contact with nature. It would discipline conduct and uplift public taste by providing a restful and decorous environment. At a time when cultural leaders felt particular concern about threats to public order, especially from "the dangerous classes," the park would serve as a gentle but effective school for citizenship. According to one genteel observer, "rude, noisy fellows," as they entered the park, became "hushed, moderate and careful"; and various of the park's supporters gleefully told the story of the saloonkeeper who came to Central Park "to see what the devil you'd got here that took off so many of my Sunday customers." "No one who has closely observed the conduct of the people who visit [Central] Park," Olmsted declared triumphantly in 1870, "can doubt that it exercises a distinctly harmonizing and refining influence upon the most unfortunate and most lawless classes of the city,—an influence favorable to courtesy, self-control, and temperance."[5]

In fact, however, there were limitations to the park's refining influence, as Olmsted himself was soon forced to acknowledge. Although Central Park proved enormously popular, attracting an average of 30,000 visitors a day for a total of ten million in the year 1871, the park lay so far uptown from New York's center of population that the great majority of citizens could afford the time and money for an excursion only on special occasions. On ordinary days the park ministered to the more prosperous classes. This situation did not greatly disturb Olmsted, since he foresaw the continued northward settlement of the city and the time when Central Park would indeed be centrally located. Olmsted regarded with much more dismay the terms by which the park was administered and maintained. In 1870 the forces of "Boss" William M. Tweed abolished the Board of Commissioners by which the genteel elite exercised independent control of the park and substituted the Department of Public Parks under the rule of Tammany Hall. Thereafter, Olmsted's conception of the park as a superbly tended work of natural art clashed with the practices of New York's local politicians, for whom the park represented a splendid opportunity for patronage and a vast, hospitable space able to accommodate multifarious uses, from fireworks displays, merry-go-rounds, and baseball fields to burial facilities for eminent figures. Olmsted and his genteel associates were derided as "the Miss Nancies of Central Park art," and their lofty visions lampooned as mere "babble in the papers and in Society Circles, about aesthetics and architecture, vistas and landscapes, the quiver of a leaf and the proper blendings of light and shade." Under such unsympathetic administrators, Olmsted discovered his high standards of public decorum mocked by both the indifference of park keepers and the wanton vandalism and disorder of visitors. The early history

The World's Columbian
Exposition

Bird's-Eye View of the World's Columbian Exposition, Chicago, 1893.

of Central Park reflected a conflict in conceptions of culture and urban recreation that would become increasingly apparent toward the end of the nineteenth century.[6]

Olmsted applied the urban pastoralism of Central Park, his first major project, to numerous other parks across the country, only to see it displaced by a second model of urban planning and recreation in his last major undertaking: the World's Columbian Exposition of 1893 in Chicago. Designed to celebrate the four hundredth anniversary of the discovery of America, the Chicago world's fair was one of the most lavish ever created. Like Central Park, the Exposition expressed the vision of a social and cultural elite eager to re-create society in its own image. A coalition of public-minded Chicago businessmen, including banker Lyman Gage, lawyer Thomas B. Bryan, banker and merchant Charles L. Hutchinson, newspaper editor Joseph G. Medill, merchant Harlow Higinbotham, and merchant and real estate promoter Potter Palmer, pooled their talents, influence, and bankrolls to mount a grandiose display which would trumpet Chicago and America's cultural achievement to all the world. To embody their vision, they turned to Chicago architect Daniel H. Burnham. As chief of construction for the fair, Burnham coordinated the efforts of the nation's most prestigious artists and architects, including landscapists Olmsted and his partner Harry Codman, architects McKim, Mead and White, Van Brunt and Howe, Peabody and Stearns, Adler and Sullivan, and Richard Morris Hunt, sculptors Daniel Chester French, Frederick MacMonnies, and Augustus Saint-Gaudens, and muralists John LaFarge, Kenyon Cox, and Elihu Vedder. To underwrite their efforts, Chicago businessmen raised ten million dollars toward the cost of the fair, which ultimately rose to an estimated forty-six million dollars. Still the fair was a bargain if one accepted Burnham's claim that after the Revolution and the Civil War it constituted the third great event of American history.[7]

Daniel H. Burnham

At an early stage in the planning of the fair, Burnham and the participating architects agreed to construct their buildings according to a unified plan and in a common idiom of neoclassicism. This consensus was easily achieved, since most of the architects, sculptors, and artists had received their formative training at the Ecole des Beaux-Arts in Paris, where they imbibed a respect for tradition, proportion, symmetry, monumentality, grandeur, and vista. The overwhelming dominance of Italian Renaissance art at the Exposition represented not only a visual preference but a cultural ideal. When Augustus Saint-Gaudens concluded one planning session by breathlessly exclaiming to Burnham, "Look here, old fellow, do you realize that this is the greatest meeting of artists since the Fifteenth Century?" he was expressing the creators' heady sense that they had embarked upon an aesthetic collaboration that would transform society. The Columbian Exposition offered architects, artists, and patrons an opportunity to construct an ideal that would purify the gross materialism of American culture, order its chaotic energies, and uplift its taste and character. Out of their united efforts, they aimed to create a monumental White City, an image of Venice purified and reborn. As an ideal, the White City would be a Dream City, rising in less than two and a half years out of the Chicago mire to flourish for a few seasons, and then in 1896 to be dismantled. On closer inspection, the gleaming white marble of the Exposition buildings turned out to be staff, a compound of plaster and fibrous binding, clothing wood and steel. Nonetheless, the fair's designers and wealthy supporters intended the lesson of the Columbian Exposition to endure: an embodiment of public order, cultural unity, and civic virtue, an animating vision of American cultural achievement for an age of disorder, strife, and vulgarity. The fair challenged Americans to join in a new cultural Renaissance.[8]

The Columbian Exposition, then, like Central Park, provided an alternative environment that expressed a strong critique of urban conditions and culture. But the remedies the two offered were radically different. While Central Park sought to distance the city by enveloping visitors in a picturesque rural retreat, the Exposition aimed to elevate the city by its example of monumental grandeur. The contrasting settings of romantic landscape and neoclassical cityscape invited quite different responses, as contemporary lithographs and photographs make clear. Central Park provided a few formal

View of the lake in
Central Park

areas including a mall and fountain where gregarious people might congregate. Most of the park, however, presented a series of rural vistas which beckoned visitors in a variety of directions and dispersed the crowds into small groups. The emphasis throughout lay upon the arrangement of natural landscape elements so that visitors would lose all sense of the city.

In contrast, the Columbian Exposition sought not to diminish the urban presence but to heighten the sense of possibility of what a city might be. Instead of submerging architectural statements in a natural order like Central Park, the Exposition accentuated them to the fullest extent possible. Visitors standing at the major focal point of the White City, the Court of Honor, were enclosed in an imperial architecture embodying a vision of order. To both east and west, they beheld a stunning ensemble of opulent buildings flanking

19

The Court of Honor,
looking west

a formal basin 2,500 feet long, rimmed with colonnades. At the far western end stood Richard Morris Hunt's monumental Administration Building, with its golden dome, recalling both the Duomo in Florence and St. Peter's in Rome. To the east rising one hundred feet above the lagoon was Daniel Chester French's colossal statue "The Republic," garbed in a Grecian toga and holding aloft an eagle perched on a globe and a liberty cap as symbols of protection and freedom. Behind the statue to the far east, separating the basin from Lake Michigan, lay the Peristyle, a series of forty-eight Corinthian columns, one for each of the states and territories, with a great triumphal arch in the center, crowned with a heroic statue of Columbus in a horse-drawn chariot. Here was an overpowering scene of classical grandeur, unity, symmetry, and vista, all presented on a monumental scale. Here was the embodiment of the genteel ideal of

The Court of Honor,
looking east

culture: "correct" and cosmopolitan, tasteful and urban, dignified and didactic. At night the splendor of the scene was further enhanced by an unprecedented battery of floodlights, using three times as much electricity as the rest of Chicago. The Exposition called upon visitors not to lose their imaginations in private contemplation as in Central Park, but to summon themselves to consciousness of public responsibilities.

Certainly the Exposition attracted a public hungry for recreation, just as Central Park had done. Paid admissions totaled 21,480,141 as people flocked from throughout the nation and abroad. Numerous commentators came away stunned by the fair's magnificent display and declared it heralded a new era of American cultural achievement. For Henry Demarest Lloyd, the fair "revealed to the people, possibilities of social beauty, utility, and harmony of which they had not been

21

The crowd at the
Columbian Exposition

able even to dream." For Henry Adams, "Chicago was the first expression of American thought as a unity." For William Dean Howells the Exposition was a vision of utopian cooperation and the attainment of a true civic life, "a foretaste of heaven."[9]

Nonetheless, the strenuous cultural demands of the fair could prove oppressive. Excited by the sublimity of the Exposition, the writer Hamlin Garland insisted that his parents leave their Dakota farm to see it for themselves. After a day devoted to the White City, passing from "one stupendous vista to another," his mother reeled under its strange magnificence. "Take me home," she pleaded to her son, bent on his errand of cultural uplift. "I can't stand any more of it."[10]

As Frederick Law Olmsted toured the White City, he made a similar, unsettling discovery: the crowds of visitors about him wore a tired, dutiful, "melancholy air" like that he had seen often on city streets and had tried to counteract with large public parks. *"More incidents of vital human gaiety wanted,"* he emphatically urged Daniel Burnham. *"Expression of the crowd too business like, common, dull, anxious and care-worn."* Olmsted suggested introducing unexpected festive elements: masqueraders, singing children, musicians, colorful peddlers—anything to enliven the scene. Why not, he continued, hire exotic figures in native costume—"varieties of 'heathen,' " Olmsted put it—from the Midway?[11]

To suggest borrowing attractions from the Midway indicated the sterility of the Exposition's conception of urban culture. For the Midway Plaisance, as it was formally called, the recreational area of the fair, had been kept carefully distinct from the White City proper and included grudgingly as a concession to public taste. The split reflected the distinction of Chicago's custodians of culture and genteel critics at large between the arts that refined and those that merely amused, those that fortified the spirit and those that gratified the senses, ultimately between those that blessed and those that cursed.[12] The effect of this polarity was to cast "high" culture in a self-consciously ministerial posture, insisting upon its own dignity, purity, nobility, and correctness, attempting to influence life while standing at a remove from it. Moving onto ever higher ground, the proponents of genteel culture abandoned the broad plains of society to the growing mass culture, which eagerly accepted the public on its own terms. Thus, to the chagrin of the fair's planners, the Midway's privately sponsored commercial attractions proved more popular than the White City's free cultural exhibits.

The Midway in effect formed a colossal sideshow, with restaurants, shops, exhibits, and theaters extending down a huge corridor, six hundred feet wide and a mile long, from the Exposition grounds westward to Washington Park. Here the Beaux-Arts neoclassicism of the Court of Honor gave way to Barnumesque eclecticism, refined order to exuberant chaos. Fairgoers threaded their way on foot or in hired chairs among a hurly-burly of exotic attractions:

Tourists on the Midway

(OPPOSITE) "Little
Egypt"

mosques and pagodas, Viennese streets and Turkish bazaars, South
Sea island huts, Irish and German castles, and Indian tepees. Tourists
gawked at the extraordinary panorama of the world's peoples:
Egyptian swordsmen and jugglers, Dahomean drummers, Sudanese
sheiks, Javanese carpenters, Hungarian gypsies, Eskimos, Chinese,
Laplanders, Swedes, Syrians, Samoans, Sioux, on and on, in the
language of the guidebooks, "from the nightsome North and the
splendid South, from the wasty West and the effete East, bringing
their manners, customs, dress, religions, legends, amusements, that we
might know them the better." Visitors were titillated by the prospect
of the World Congress of Beauty with "40 Ladies from 40 Nations,"
in reality an exhibition of native costumes. They pushed into the
Streets of Cairo, the Algerian Village, and the Persian Palace of Eros

"Been to see the dancing girls"

"Been to see the
dancing girls"

to watch entranced as "Little Egypt," and her colleagues and competitors, performed the "danse du ventre," popularly known as the hootchy-kootchy. The "suggestively lascivious contorting of the abdominal muscles" was denounced by scandalized moralists as "extremely ungraceful and almost shockingly disgusting"; but as the illustrator E. W. Kemble observed, many men left the spectacle with noticeably unoutraged expressions. The Midway, in short, offered a far different conception of cultural cosmopolitanism than the Court of Honor, one oriented not to the ordered and refined past but to the heterogeneous and boisterous present. Appropriately, the dominant monument of the Midway was no allegorical figure of civic virtue in classical garb like French's statue "The Republic," but the gigantic, spare steel wheel designed by George W. G. Ferris especially for the Exposition, a striking instance of modern machine engineering in the service of pleasure. Visitors could without charge climb a stairway inside French's statue to view the Court of Honor from her uplifting perspective; for fifty cents, however, they could purchase two revolutions in the Ferris Wheel carrying them two and a half times as high, where they gazed beyond the static ideal of the White City to the dynamic, urban, industrial, ethnically diverse world of the city of Chicago.[13]

As historians have often noted, the White City exerted a considerable influence upon American architecture in general and upon urban planning in the "City Beautiful" movement. The monumental classicism of the Exposition would dominate public building into the 1930s, and Daniel Burnham would personally play a key role in devising unified city plans for Chicago, Washington, San Francisco, and Cleveland, with many others following his example. Far less noted but also significant was the legacy of the Midway. It stimulated a new industry of traveling carnival shows and new attractions for popular resorts. It suggested an entirely different model of democratic urban recreation from either Central Park or the White City, a park designed not according to the civic values of cultural elites but according to the commercial values of entrepreneurs determined to attract a mass audience. The new "amusement parks" which

The Ferris Wheel

emerged at the turn of the century would be the result—parks which, as their name suggests, sought frankly to entertain rather than to uplift. Their character deserves more searching examination than it has generally received, for these amusement parks expressed changes in American culture that monuments such as the White City attempted to suppress. To understand their full significance, we need to go to the undisputed capital of amusement at the turn of the century, Coney Island.

Directly south of Brooklyn and nine miles from Manhattan, Coney Island had begun attracting visitors in the early nineteenth century. The first hotel, the Coney Island House, was built in 1829, and in the antebellum period the area slowly acquired a few restaurants, bathhouses, and barrooms, and a small side-wheel steamboat service linking the Island's West End to New York.[14]

As Coney Island developed, it reflected the tensions in the larger culture. Standing at a comfortable remove from New York, Coney lured wealthier customers eager for seaside seclusion. They amused themselves strolling on the beach and wading in the surf, digging clams or hunting for snipe and duck, lounging in porch chairs and dining on seafood. Coney Island's combination of seclusion and proximity to New York also attracted a rougher element who demanded gamier amusement. As early as the 1860s, Norton's Point at the western end had become a haven for gamblers, confidence men, pickpockets, roughnecks, and prostitutes, who could ply their trades upon recreation seekers beyond the reach of New York and Brooklyn officials. Such elements constituted the counterculture of Victorian America; their activities, an inversion of genteel cultural norms.

In the postwar decades investors seized upon the possibilities of Coney Island as a resort and poured money into it. The antiquated steamer was superseded by an increasing number of steamboat and railroad lines, and a colorful array of fancifully palatial hotels rose along the beach. In an effort to overcome Coney's tarnished reputation, promoters coined new names for the Island's various sections. The infamous Norton's Point, rechristened the West End, faded in prominence as rivals sprang up to the east, assuming new identities as West Brighton, Brighton Beach, and Manhattan Beach.

Brighton Beach and Manhattan Beach harbored the greatest pretensions to respectability and managed most successfully to secede from the name and taint of Coney Island; hence they will play little role in this account. Under the sponsorship of the railroad and real estate magnate Austin Corbin, Manhattan Beach boasted the most

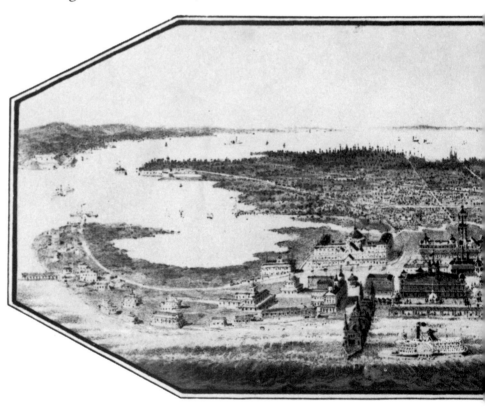

Coney Island in the 1880s

lavish accommodations and exclusive clientele. Corbin constructed the New York & Manhattan Beach Railway in 1876–77 so that New York nabobs could travel in an hour from midtown Manhattan directly to his stylish new hotels, the Manhattan Beach (1877) and, soon after, the Oriental (1880), the latter rising four stories and capped by exotic minarets.

As Corbin shaped Manhattan Beach, his neighbor to the west, William A. Engeman, molded Brighton Beach. Engeman, who had previously made a fortune selling mules to the federal government during the Civil War, seized upon the new opportunities for profit in amusement. Patiently acquiring widely scattered land rights to the area, by 1878 he presided over the two-story Brighton Beach Bathing Pavilion and its famous Iron Pier, and the Brighton Beach Hotel, which offered broad verandas, beds of flowers, the "seclusion and

quietude of a family hotel of the first order," and private railroad connections to New York City.[15]

Nonetheless, the vital center of Coney Island remained West Brighton, the site of the original Coney Island House and the basis of modern Coney, whose name it would soon reassume. Even as early as the 1870s West Brighton contained too many diverse establishments to fall under the control of a single figure. As developers competed with one another, they aimed not for the elegance of Manhattan Beach or the secluded domesticity of Brighton; rather they catered to the multitude. To this end they expanded the capacity

West Brighton and the Elephant Hotel

of traditional seaside amusements to the utmost and introduced alluring new ones. Thus when Andrew R. Culver built the Prospect Park & Coney Island Railroad to carry visitors to West Brighton at thirty-five cents a head, he also devised attractions to draw and keep them there. The Culver Line terminal opened onto the ornamental Culver Plaza, where tourists were frequently greeted with band concerts. By taking only a few more steps they could reach the base of his 300-foot-high Iron Tower, a gigantic souvenir of the Philadelphia Centennial Exposition of 1876, with two steam elevators to carry customers to an observation platform.

Culver and others built hotels, restaurants, and other facilities designed to accommodate guests by the thousands. The fact that their advertised capacities may be inflated merely confirms their orientation toward quantity. The Sea Beach Palace (1879) claimed to be able to serve 15,000 diners at a sitting and house 10,000 guests overnight. The West Brighton Hotel boasted a kitchen that could serve 8,000 people daily. Charles Feltman's Ocean Pavilion (1874) proclaimed itself the largest building on Coney Island, with rooms for 20,000 guests, a ballroom for 3,000 dancers, and a piazza for 5,000 more onlookers. In addition, Feltman opened in 1878 a 1,000-foot-long Iron Pier, with space for dancing, various game and food stands, and 1,200 bath lockers. By these and other efforts West Brighton monopolized Coney Island tourism. Of an estimated 60,000 visitors to Coney Island on a warm Sunday in 1878, 50,000 spent their time and money at West Brighton.

One further hotel built in 1882 brought countless additional thousands to the area even though it contained relatively few rooms. This was the Elephant, an immense sculpture made out of wood and covered with tin, with spiral staircases in its hind legs, a diorama and a cigar store in its front legs, a shopping mall and guest rooms in its body, and an observatory in its head. A trip to the Elephant Hotel quickly became an essential part of the Coney Island visitor's itinerary, and the phrase "seeing the elephant," often accompanied by a broad wink, became a euphemism for illicit pleasures.

For illicit as well as licit pleasures still flourished at West Brighton even if Brighton Beach and Manhattan Beach professed loftier standards. Around the large hotels, restaurants, and bathing pavilions clustered innumerable saloons, variety shows, bands, shooting galleries, sideshows, catchpenny games, food vendors, crayon portraitists, photographers, fortune tellers, as well as the con men, whores, and thugs of old. Through the 1880s and early 1890s such enterprises flourished under the approving eye of local political boss John Y. McKane. As a result of his administration, the community quickly won the sobriquet "Sodom by the Sea" and the fervid denunciations of preachers, legislators, journalists, and reformers. However, it was not these forces so much as McKane's political foes who finally brought him to account and sent him to Sing Sing in 1894 on a conviction of election fraud. Contemporaneous with McKane's departure, in 1893 and 1895 fires ravaged the entertainment section of West Brighton. With the aid of these purifying agents, the stage was set for the beginning of a new era at Coney Island.

In McKane's wake a number of entrepreneurs, following the lead of a young local businessman named George C. Tilyou, sought to redeem Coney Island's corrupt image. Together they transformed the resort, devising elaborate new attractions and, beginning in 1895, enclosing them in separate amusement parks. These parks arose to challenge one another in quick succession. First Captain Paul Boyton's Sea Lion Park with its dramatic water slide, Shoot-the-Chutes; then in 1897 George Tilyou's Steeplechase Park, named for the elaborate mechanical racetrack that ringed its borders. By 1903 two men brought by Tilyou to Coney Island, Frederic Thompson and Elmer "Skip" Dundy, bought Sea Lion Park from Boyton and created a spectacular new amusement center, Luna Park. Their achievement stimulated a final challenger, William H. Reynolds's Dreamland, which imitated many of Luna's attractions and opened across the street in 1904.

In transforming Coney Island, the creators of these amusement parks were animated more by pecuniary interest than reformist zeal. As one contemporary put it, they discovered that "vice does not

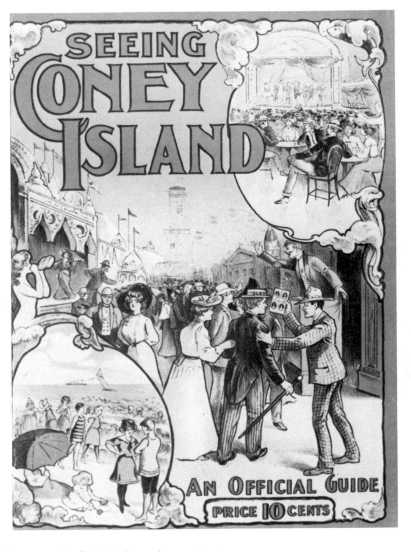

pay as well as decency."[16] They realized that Coney's greatest potential lay not in corruptly defying the genteel culture as McKane had done but in providing a respectable alternative to it with exciting, uninhibited amusement. Contemporaneous with other amusement entrepreneurs in various fields—minstrelsy, the circus, vaudeville, variety shows, the movies—they sensed the emergence of a large new

35

heterogeneous audience who simultaneously desired the assurance of "wholesome" entertainment and hungered for forms and themes that satisfied their taste for sensory appeal and emotional release. New York's population of white-collar workers and their families was expanding enormously, creating both a larger mass audience for amusement and, as urban congestion increased, a greater need for it. By the turn of the century commercial entertainments were sweeping the urban middle class and even penetrating the lives of the working class, despite the fact that most manual laborers still worked just under ten hours a day, six days a week, and, barring layoffs, fifty-two weeks a year for annual earnings of approximately $600. Although for poorer individuals and families domestic-centered events such as birthdays, weddings, and holidays remained the principal recreations, these were increasingly supplemented by commercial amusements such as dance halls, music halls, neighborhood theaters, vaudeville houses, the movies, and amusement parks. A wide range of attractions was increasingly available, offering in return for modest admission fees the pleasures of a partial holiday whenever one could take it, weekdays and Sundays, daytimes and evenings, many on a "continuous performance" basis.

The response to the establishment of Coney's amusement parks at the turn of the century was immediate and overwhelming. The "New Coney Island," so reporters and publicists hailed it, quickly achieved nationwide fame. It emerged as a popular countertype to Chicago's White City, an alternative model of urban recreation. Thus, it attracted both unprecedented crowds and widespread critical attention in the period up to 1920. As visitors thronged to Coney from New York and the nation, journalists, critics, photographers, and painters followed them closely, eager to observe their behavior and to confront this new cultural phenomenon at first hand. To arrive at our own understanding of Coney Island, we need to retrace the steps of these visitors and then of the critics and to examine the responses of both groups. In so doing, we may rediscover not only the meaning Coney Island held for its visitors but its significance for American culture as a whole.

Although the subway did not extend all the way to Coney Island until 1920, turn-of-the-century visitors made their way by a variety of routes and often a combination of conveyances. These included excursion boats, ferryboats, railroads, elevated trains, electric trolleys, subway trains, horsecars, hackney carriages, automobiles, and bicycles. The cheapest fare to the resort in the early 1890s had been forty cents, fifty for a steamer; but improvements in rapid transit beginning with the nickel trolley ride to Coney in 1895 forced these prices down and brought the excursion within the means of the great multitude. The time required for the journey obviously varied greatly depending upon the route and means one took, but the construction of new bridges and tunnels linking New York's boroughs combined with the speed of elevated trains, railroads, and subways all made Coney's amusement parks widely accessible. Express trains from Brooklyn Bridge, for example, reportedly reached the gates of Luna Park in only thirty-two minutes.

Coney Island's amusement parks were open from May until early September, and in the heat of the summer the crush of visitors reached staggering proportions. Hordes of pleasure seekers flocked to the resort whenever they had leisure, often in hours snatched after work during the week and especially on Sundays and holidays. Coney no longer reckoned its customers merely in the thousands. Press agents declared the multitudes numbered as many as 200,000 on a single day, and Luna Park claimed five million paid admissions in a season. In the proud phrase of Luna's manager, Frederic Thompson, Coney Island was in the business of "amusing the million."[17] The resort offered amusement on a scale unprecedented in American history. Here the new mass culture was not a vague abstraction but a tangible reality.

Impressed by the extraordinary size of the crowds at Coney, turn-of-the-century observers were equally struck by their diversity. Readers accustomed to the more informal standards of dress of our own time may mistake the jackets, ties, hats, dresses, and parasols in old photographs as evidence of an elite clientele. However, these constituted the public fashion of the day observed by all classes, particularly on special outings. Closer inspection indicates what various observers confirm: Coney Island drew upon all social classes and especially upon the rising middle class and the more prosperous working-class visitors, salesmen, clerks, tradesmen, secretaries, shop attendants, laborers, and the like.

Coney Island accommodated purses of varying sizes. Most individual attractions at Coney Island charged ten cents apiece. Sometimes, however, there were bargains; in 1905 Steeplechase Park began offering a combination ticket of twenty-five rides for twenty-five cents. The nickels and dimes quickly mounted up, and many customers undoubtedly spent more money than they initially intended. One journalist provided an indication of what a day at Coney might cost a couple when he overheard the conversation of two young women comparing notes on their escorts' largesse:

"What sort of time did you have?"

"Great. He blew in $5.00 on the blow out."

"You beat me again. My chump only spent $2.55."

Yet by no means was it necessary to spend anywhere near this much to participate in Coney Island's amusement. Indeed, some who could afford no more than carfare still came to Coney "merely for the joy of mixing with the crowds on the public street and catching the live sense of humanity and of good humor that is everywhere." Others might put aside a little money for a special excursion to Coney as later generations would for a summer vacation. Two separately conducted surveys of working-class families in Manhattan around 1905 found outings to Coney Island once or twice a summer prominently mentioned, even though these people had scant budgets for recreation.[18]

In addition to families, young men and women came by themselves to Coney, saving whatever spending money they could, sometimes skipping lunches and walking to work in order to have enough for a trip to the resort. Coney offered pleasures infinitely more thrilling than the dominant youthful pastimes of sitting on the front steps or hanging around on the street. Young working-class women in particular could plan to spend no more than the cost of their transportation, since they quickly attracted escorts eager to "treat."[19]

Increasingly, too, Coney Island reflected the changing ethnic character of Brooklyn, Manhattan, and the greater New York area. Led by newcomers from Italy and Eastern Europe, immigration mounted to unprecedented proportions during this period. According to one government survey, New York's immigrant population increased by well over 400,000 in each of the last two decades of the nineteenth century. By the turn of the century, immigrants constituted a majority of adults both in Manhattan and in Brooklyn. The ranks of foreign-born swelled by an additional 942,000 in the first decade of the twentieth century and roughly another 400,000 by 1920.[20] Soon Irish, Germans, Italians, Eastern European Jews, and other groups were joining Anglo-Saxon Americans in pursuit of pleasure. Coney Island provided attractions and generated a sense of festivity in many respects familiar to frequenters of, say, New York's Italian street festivals, band concerts, and theaters, or to celebrants of Purim and patrons of the Yiddish theater. At the same time, the resort lifted visitors beyond the confines of home and neighborhood, of foreign languages and folkways. For immigrants and especially for their children, notoriously eager to assimilate, Coney Island provided a means to participate in mainstream American culture on an equal footing. Far more immediately and successfully than agents of the genteel culture, Coney's amusement parks and other institutions of the new mass culture incorporated immigrants and working-class groups into their forms and values.

Coney Island's development as a summer resort for the multitude coincided with the lifting of various post office restrictions on the mailing of picture postcards at the turn of the century, and many visitors delighted in buying either black-and-white or colored views of Coney Island scenes. They both collected them as personal souvenirs and sent them to friends and relatives back in the city and elsewhere as tokens of their excursions. Such postcards offered a way to celebrate one's outing as a step outside the everyday world. Messages like "Margaret and I are down here having lots of fun," and "Greet-

Passengers arriving at steel pier, Coney Island, 1906

ings to all from Coney Island," so familiar to us now, constituted a radical break with the older epistolary style in favor of a clipped new form of communication for an age of mass leisure. In effect, they exclaimed simply that the writer was at Coney Island on a holiday and thoroughly enjoying himself, while thinking of others—a fine balance of egotism and altruism. One card dispensed with a picture entirely in favor of the profanely emphatic printed declaration to which the sender needed only to sign his name: I AM HAVING A H . . . OF A GOOD TIME AT CONEY ISLAND.[21]

As such postcards suggest, an essential element of Coney Island's appeal for virtually all its visitors was the contrast it offered to conventional society, everyday routine, and dominant cultural authorities. Though traces of class and ethnic backgrounds still clung to Coney Island's amusement seekers, in arriving at the resort they crossed a critical threshold, entering a world apart from ordinary life, prevailing social structures and positions. Designers of both Central Park and the Columbian Exposition had sought to create environments that would ultimately reinforce existing social structures and discipline public life. Coney Island, by contrast, provided an area in which visitors were temporarily freed from normative demands. As they disembarked from ferryboats with fanciful names like *Pegasus,* or walked toward the amusement parks along Surf Avenue, they felt themselves passing into a special realm of exciting possibility, a distinctive milieu that encouraged types of behavior and social interaction that in other contexts would have been regarded askance. Commentators often observed, "Coney Island has a code of conduct which is all her own."[22] The amusement center suspended conventional situational proprieties. It encouraged visitors to shed momentarily their accustomed roles and status. Coney offered a relatively "loose," unregulated social situation which contrasted markedly with the high degree of social attentiveness and decorum demanded in most other public activities. It broke down the sense of rigidity that dominated so much of the life of American cities at the turn of the century and lessened personal restraints. The kind of civil inattention prevalent in other public places was not nearly so strictly observed here. Coney's sense of conviviality was contagious. Visitors displayed open interest in one another's activities and fed upon their mutual hilarity. Strangers frequently fell into conversation. In what critics increasingly charged was an impersonal society, Coney Island provided a welcome institution for public fellowship.

The relaxation of conventional proprieties made Coney Island especially popular with young men and women. The middle-class ideal as described in etiquette books of the period placed severe restraints on the circumstances under which a man might presume even to tip his hat to a woman in public; and certainly such books would never approve a gentleman intruding himself upon a lady with whom he was unacquainted. The social codes of the working class were less formal, but many families observed a strict etiquette of courting, monitoring the activities of their daughters especially and insisting upon the presence of a chaperon, if need be a child, when male callers came to the home. In such circumstances, as one New Yorker from an immigrant working-class family later recalled, for the young, ironically, "privacy could be had only in public."[23] Sidewalks, public parks, dance halls, and amusement parks offered opportunities to meet and enjoy the company of the opposite sex away from familial scrutiny. At Coney Island in particular, unattached young men and women easily struck up acquaintanceships for the day or evening. According to Coney Island folklore, some couples even married on the spot. The freedom of anonymity together with the holiday atmosphere of the resort encouraged intimacy and an easing of inhibitions and permitted couples to display their affections in public.

Coney Island thus offered strikingly visible expression of major shifts in sexual mores traditionally associated with the 1920s but beginning to take place at this time. Postcards like the one of a couple warmly embracing on the beach celebrated the sexual freedom the resort afforded. Various amusements contrived to lift women's skirts and reveal their legs and underclothing, while numerous others provided opportunities for intimate physical contact. Slow, scenic rides through tunnels and caves offered abundant occasions for

"spooning" and "petting," to use the language of the day. Other, more vigorous rides worked less subtly, throwing couples into each other's arms. One ride, the "Cannon Coaster," articulated the appeal of many similar attractions in advertising: WILL SHE THROW HER ARMS AROUND YOUR NECK AND YELL? WELL, I GUESS, YES! For another attraction, the "Barrel of Love," in which passengers were strapped into seats in a gently revolving drum, a sign exclaimed, "Talk about love in a cottage! This has it beat a mile."[24]

One may gather additional hints of the way Coney Island loosened the rigors of a structured society simply by contrasting scenes at the resort with city street scenes of the same period. In turn-of-the-century photographs of urban life, we see people of all classes proceeding quickly and unostentatiously about their business. Even in situations in which they wished to invite public notice, such as New York's "Easter parade" along Fifth Avenue in front of St. Patrick's, participants maintained a strong situational "presence" and sense of propriety that restrained self-dramatizing gestures or intense personal interaction. Keenly interested in the social drama about them and their potential part in it, they nonetheless held them-

43

selves in check and assumed fairly rigid postures. Not simply their dress but their whole demeanor remained formal.

From the beginning of Coney Island's history as a resort a strong element of its appeal lay in the way it permitted a respite from such formal, highly regulated social situations. Coney's initial attraction, the beach, furnished an occasion for a relaxation of proprieties. The most obvious aspect of this "looseness," the lack of social rigidity and situational "presence," was clothing. Notions of propriety of dress have clearly changed enormously since the turn of the century, so that to a modern reader the fashion of dress visitors wore even on Coney Island's beaches may appear rather formal. But it is important to look at the photographs of turn-of-the-century Coney Island, not according to present conventions, but in light of the prevailing standards of the day. Modest as they may appear to our eyes, the bathing

Easter formality on Fifth Avenue, 1904

suits of the time were in every sense looser than customary street wear. Not only did they expose more of the wearer's body, but they also encouraged freer deportment in general. One 1890s commentator, fascinated by this transformation of behavior, observed: "The haughty dowager, the exquisite maid, the formal-minded matron, the pompous buck, the pretty dandy, don with their unconstricting garb of bath-flannels, a devil-may-care disregard for the modes and conventions of fashion that reminds one strongly of [Herodotus'] comment on the close relation between womanly pudicity and its outer garb."[25]

Period photographs of Coney Island bathers support this observation. Subjects characteristically stand, sit on the beach, or wade in the surf in noticeably more relaxed postures than pedestrians on city streets. They appear more animated and engrossed in their own

Summer informality at Coney Island, 1913

Posing in front of the
iron pier, 1903

particular pleasures, less concerned with paying deferential respect
to the gathering as a whole. In some photographs bathers call explicit
attention to the freedom Coney Island permitted by striking broad,
dramatic poses and exuberantly mugging for the camera. Lifting and
supporting one another, arms and bodies interlinked, they display
a sense of solidarity and mutual pleasure in the release of social
restraints. A stereoscopic view of 1897 entitled "Ah, there! Coney
Island" celebrated particularly the sexual aspect of this freedom, the

"naughtiness" of violating customary proprieties. Five young women raise the hems of their bathing dresses and thrust out their buttocks as they grin coquettishly toward the viewer. Here was a far different notion of recreation than Olmsted or Burnham had imagined.

This liberating social setting was by no means limited to the beach. Indeed, as Coney Island's attractions proliferated and crowds increased, journalists observed ironically that one could spend a day at the resort and never see the water. As visitors entered the amuse-

CONEY ISLAND BEACH
Copyright
IRVING UNDER

ment area, they encountered an environmental phantasmagoria, combining characteristics of the beer garden, county fair, Chicago Midway, vaudeville, and circus. Photographs give some indication of this environment, but they alone cannot do it justice. We must try to imagine the smells of circus animals, the taste of hot dogs, beer, and seafood, the jostle of surrounding revelers, the speed and jolts of amusement rides, and, what especially impressed observers, the din of barkers, brass bands, roller coasters, merry-go-rounds, shooting galleries, and hundreds of other attractions—above all, the shouts and laughter of the crowd itself. All combined to create the holiday atmosphere of Coney Island, an invitation to collective gaiety and release. Coney Island plunged visitors into a powerful kinesthetic experience that, like the surf itself, overturned conventional restraints, washed away everyday concerns, buoyed and buffeted participants as they submitted to its sway.

As a city of festivity and play, Coney Island challenged conventional categories of social description. It appeared to be a new kind of cultural institution, and commentators groped for analogies

49

to describe it: "an almost uninterrupted French *fête*," "a medieval street fair," a "fiesta and mardi-gras," a "charivari," and, again and again, a "carnival."[26]

The analogy of carnival and similar festivals is an extremely illuminating one. It helps explain the special appeal of Coney Island for Americans at the turn of the century and offers important clues to the resort's cultural significance. Carnivals and other seasonal feasts and festivals, such as Saturnalia and the Feast of Fools, have served in a number of pre-industrial cultures as occasions in which customary roles are reversed, hierarchies overturned, and penalties suspended. Often donning masks and costumes, all the members of the community join in extravagant buffoonery and merrymaking. Coney Island appeared to have institutionalized the carnival spirit for a culture that lacked a carnival tradition, but Coney located its festivity not in time as a special moment on the calendar but in space as a special place on the map. By creating its own version of carnival, Coney Island tested and transformed accustomed social roles and values. It attracted people because of the way in which it mocked the established social order. Coney Island in effect declared a moral holiday for all who entered its gates. Against the values of thrift, sobriety, industry, and ambition, it encouraged extravagance, gaiety, abandon, revelry. Coney Island signaled the rise of a new mass culture no longer deferential to genteel tastes and values, which demanded a democratic resort of its own. It served as a Feast of Fools for an urban-industrial society.[27]

Beginning with the various sideshows and exhibits along Coney Island's main promenade, the Bowery, the tourists entered into this carnival world. As in traditional carnivals and fairs, the grotesque was prominently represented, symbolizing the exaggerated and excessive character of Coney Island as a whole. Midgets, giants, fat ladies, and ape-men were both stigmatized and honored as freaks. They fascinated spectators in the way they displayed themselves openly as exceptions to the rules of the conventional world. Their grotesque presences heightened the visitors' sense that they had penetrated a marvelous realm of transformation, subject to laws all its own. The

(OPPOSITE) Crowds on Coney Island's Bowery, 1903

50

popular distorting mirrors furnished the illusion that the spectators themselves had become freaks. Thus Coney Island seemed charged with a magical power to transmute customary appearances into fluid new possibilities.[28]

Besides freaks of nature, Coney Island further mocked the humdrum character of the larger society by presenting freaks of culture. Only two years after the Columbian Exposition, Coney boasted its own "Streets of Cairo." Visitors stared at camels and warily fed elephants, not in a circus setting but as participants in a drama that attempted within its means to suggest the mysteries of the Orient. Women and especially men clustered eagerly before canopied booths where barkers exclaimed over the allure of "Little Egypt" and other practitioners of the "danse du ventre": *This way for the Streets of Cairo! One hundred and fifty Oriental beauties! The warmest spectacle on earth! See her dance the Hootchy-Kootchy! Anywhere else but in the ocean breezes of Coney Island she would be consumed by her own fire! Don't rush! Don't crowd! Plenty of seats for all!*[29]

(OPPOSITE) Coney Island Freak Show, 1908

(ABOVE, RIGHT) Feeding the elephant, 1897

(RIGHT) "The Original Turkish Harem," 1896

Coney Island performer,
1896

Such performers could exert a captivating spell. Dressed in a richly ornamented costume, sensuously swaying to the music of finger cymbals as she posed for the photographer, a dancer quickly drew a cluster of entranced spectators. Using the boardwalk as a bare stage, by her powerfully theatrical presence and gesture she transported her audience beyond routine surroundings and lured them toward the seraglio within.

Steeplechase, Luna Park, Dreamland, the three great enclosed amusement parks that sprang up at the turn of the century, were elaborate constructions designed to heighten Coney Island's own version of carnival. Like the "Streets of Cairo" and other attractions but on a much grander scale, they borrowed freely from the Columbian Exposition and other fairs to create, in effect, a White City for the multitude, a fantastic fair for the common man. They formed the heart of the "New Coney Island" that became a center of cultural expression and of critical debate. We will want to examine them closely.

T he founder of Steeplechase Park, George C. Tilyou, was one of the millions who thronged the Chicago Midway in the summer of 1893. At the time, Tilyou's parents ran a small hotel at Coney Island, and he and his father managed a vaudeville theater. Even though the younger Tilyou was in Chicago on his honeymoon, he viewed the spectacle with more than romantic eyes—he studied it with the shrewd discernment of an impresario. The great Ferris Wheel particularly attracted him and he tried to buy it. When he learned that it had already been sold, he responded like a true showman. He ordered another wheel, half the size, hurried back to Coney, rented a plot of land, and put up a sign boldly announcing, "On This Site Will Be Erected the World's Largest Ferris Wheel." Soon he installed a wheel and grouped various other amusements around it.

When Paul Boyton opened the first enclosed amusement park, Sea Lion Park, in 1895, Tilyou saw another innovation to emulate. A modest venture by later standards, Boyton's park had a pronounced aquatic theme with forty trained sea lions, water races, an old-mill water ride, and the popular water slide in flat-bottomed boats, Shoot-the-Chutes, emptying into a lagoon. Tilyou countered by unveiling

George C. Tilyou

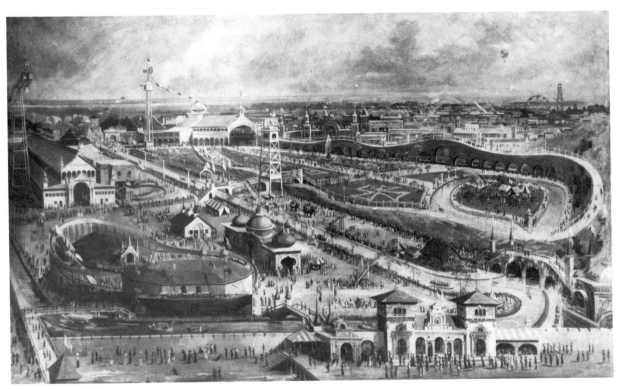

Steeplechase Park

Steeplechase Park in 1897, an elaborate collection of attractions in a fifteen-acre enclosure, ringed by the gravity-powered steeplechase race that gave the park its name. By enclosing the park from the rest of Coney Island, Tilyou both excluded unsavory elements who might deter his customers and monopolized patrons' business himself.

One does not expect showmen to divulge their formulas for success—or even necessarily to be fully conscious of them. So it is not surprising that George Tilyou maintained that "any success in the amusement business is unaccountable." But when pressed by a journalist, he cogently described the appeal he sought to satisfy: "what attracts the crowd is the wearied mind's demand for relief in unconsidered muscular action." "We Americans," Tilyou continued, "want either to be thrilled or amused, and we are ready to pay well for either sensation."[30]

Steeplechase was thus designed to provide a series of active, intense amusements that would totally involve its patrons and sweep them away from everyday concerns and restraints. As George Tilyou's son Edward remarked a few years later, amusement parks provided "a gigantic laboratory of human nature" in which people "cut loose from repressions and restrictions, and act pretty much as they feel like acting—since everyone else is doing the same thing." In Coney's permissive environment customers felt a giddy sense of irresponsibility. Among the most popular attractions, according to the younger Tilyou, were booths with imitation china dishes, objects to throw at them, and a sign: "If you can't break up your own home, break up ours!" Thus encouraged, Coney Island visitors exuberantly shed the roles of the larger world. Factory "girls," Edward Tilyou noted, pretended they occupied loftier positions and played the parts of stenographers and private secretaries for a day; and a Brooklyn shopkeeper would don her best clothes and act the part of a *grande dame.* More dramatically, a prim-looking "schoolma'am," accustomed to curbing the childish excesses of others, surrendered to her own at Coney Island and walked fully dressed into the sea. "It has been a hard year at school," she afterward explained, "and when I saw the big crowd here, everyone with the brakes off, the spirit of the place got the better of me." In her impulse toward childish release, she was not alone. "Most people," Edward Tilyou shrewdly observed, "look back on childhood as the happiest period of their lives. They may be mistaken, but this is the mental attitude they like to adopt."[31]

Steeplechase Park's various attractions catered to such desires. Instead of games of competitive skill, which demanded self-control, Steeplechase emphasized games of theatricality and of vertigo, which encouraged participants to shed self-consciousness and surrender to a spirit of reckless, exuberant play.[32] The popular Steeplechase race, for example, was essentially a hobbyhorse for adults, which provided a simple but giddy sense of transport as the mechanical steeds galloped along their inclined tracks. The "Wedding Ring," a great wooden circle suspended from a center pole, applied the principle of a playground swing to a ride that accommo-

dated up to seventy customers at once. Similarly, the human "roulette
wheel," which like a gigantic toy delighted both riders and spectators,
set passengers whirling and sprawling out from its center by centrif-
ugal force.

Steeplechase encouraged visitors to see themselves as participants
in a human comedy. George Tilyou proudly proclaimed his park as
"Steeplechase—the Funny Place" and adopted as its emblem the
huge grinning "Funny Face." A grotesque, vaguely diabolical jester,
it served as a fitting image for Steeplechase: a promise of the irrespon-
sible hilarity visitors hoped to experience within. Steeplechase installed a number of devices designed to give patrons the opportunity
to play the fool. In addition to its various rides, Steeplechase provided
"stunts" designed to catch people off guard. Visitors entering the
park from the ocean side had to pass through the "Barrel of Fun,"
a huge, slowly revolving cylinder which frequently rolled patrons off
their feet and brought strangers into sudden, intimate contact. Similarly, the main lobby of Steeplechase led customers inescapably to

the "Blowhole Theater," where concealed compressed-air jets sent hats flying and skirts shooting upward. Equally important, Steeplechase attempted to satisfy the pleasure people derived from seeing others made foolish. Erstwhile victims were encouraged to sit in the "Laughing Gallery" and act as spectators for those who followed. In this way, a major attraction of Steeplechase was simply the sanctioned opportunity to witness the wholesale violation of dominant social proprieties. Momentary disorientation, intimate exposure, physical contact with strangers, pratfalls, public humiliation—conditions that in other circumstances might have been excruciating—became richly entertaining. The laughter of participants and spectators testified to their sense of release.

Just as Tilyou borrowed from the Chicago Midway with his Ferris Wheel, so he continued to draw upon other fairs for new attractions. In 1901 he visited the Pan-American Exposition in Buffalo, New York, and was captivated by the dramatic cyclorama, "A Trip to the Moon." Here visitors entered a spaceship in the middle of a large building for an imaginary ride to the moon. Peering out of portholes, they beheld a series of shifting images that gave the illusion of a flight into space, a sense reinforced by the rocking of the ship itself. After supposedly landing on the moon, passengers left the spaceship to explore its caverns and grottoes, where they met giants and midgets in moon-men costumes, the Man in the Moon upon his throne, and dancing moon maidens, who pressed bits of green cheese upon them as souvenirs of the lunar voyage. The "Trip to the Moon" was thus an especially elaborate ride promoting a sense of fantasy and escape. Tilyou brought both the cyclorama and its creators, Frederic Thompson and Skip Dundy, back to Steeplechase, where their amusements continued to astound the crowds.

After the 1902 season, however, Thompson and Dundy left Tilyou to create their own amusement park as a rival of Steeplechase. They bought Paul Boyton's Sea Lion Park, tore down all its attractions except for Shoot-the-Chutes and its lagoon, and erected in their stead the most ambitious amusement center in the history of Coney Island, Luna Park.

LUNA PARK

THE HEART OF CONEY ISLAND

LUNA PARK

THOMPSON & DUNDY

As about 45,000 men, women, and children streamed toward Luna Park on opening night in May 1903, according to one reporter, they stopped, "rubbed their eyes, and stood in wonder and pinched themselves." They stood at the imposing gates of what appeared to be a dream city, a mysterious palace of play. Once inside, they discovered, in the words of a second journalist, "an enchanted, storybook land of trellises, columns, domes, minarets, lagoons, and lofty aërial flights. And everywhere was life—a pageant of happy people; and everywhere was color—a wide harmony of orange and white and gold. . . . It was a world removed—shut away from the sordid clatter and turmoil of the streets."[33]

A former architectural student, Thompson more than any other figure of the period realized the importance of architecture in popular amusement. He understood that a collection of individually ingenious attractions was not enough for an amusement park to succeed. The spirit of carnival needed to be sustained by a joyful, consummately theatrical setting. In an era of architectural eclecticism, Thompson borrowed freely from a variety of sources and transformed them for his own purposes. Abandoning conventional standards, he adopted what he thought best in "Free Renaissance," using "all the license in the world" and injecting into everything he did "the graceful, romantic curves of the Oriental." Throughout, Thompson indulged in rich ornament and stylistic flights of fancy to create an environment of effervescent lightness, heightened symbolism, and festive gaiety in a style that defied traditional nomenclature; one is tempted to call it Super-Saracenic or Oriental Orgasmic.[34]

Frederic Thompson

(OPPOSITE) Entrance to Luna Park

The contrast with the Columbian Exposition was especially striking. In its neoclassical formalism, the Exposition represented an architecture of responsibility; here, however, was an architecture of pleasure. The Columbian Exposition preached discipline; Luna Park invited release. Constructed out of the same impermanent plaster materials as the White City, Luna's buildings achieved monumentality without oppressiveness, grandeur without solemnity. The amusement park threw off all sense of restraint to indulge in an orgy of ebullient forms, bright colors, and sumptuous ornament. Luna represented a

63

kind of architectural "Little Egypt," deliciously sensuous, voluptuously Oriental, enticingly dynamic. Like the belly dancer, it pulsated with irresistible vitality. A succession of arches, a profusion of towers, turrets, and flags, and an abundance of detail combined to create a propulsive sense of rhythm. One could not stand detached from the spectacle and absorb it all. It extended an invitation for the observer to become an active participant. Various elements constantly competed for attention. In contrast to both the pastoralism of Central Park and the formalism of the Columbian Exposition, Luna Park presented a complex and dynamic order intended to stimulate visitors, even to overwhelm them. It promised not repose but activity, not stability but transformation. Its sinuous organic forms suggested a world in flux, inhabited by fantastic sculptured animals, like the dolphin fountain at the base of Luna's main tower and the huge winged griffins that flanked "The Dragon's Gorge"—grotesque spirits of metamorphosis.

The result was to make Luna Park a gigantic stage set that engulfed visitors in new roles. With a trip to Coney and a ten-cent admission fee visitors exchanged the dingy banality of city streets and the pompous sobriety of public buildings for a colorful holiday world. Arriving as separate, isolated figures, they became actors in a vast, collective comedy. The flamboyantly expressive surroundings had the effect of garbing customers in costumes and eliciting their own theatricality. At various moments on rides they might briefly grab the spotlight and attract the attention of the multitude; at other times they might sit in the balconies and watch their fellow revelers. The lines between spectator and performer, between professional entertainer and seeker of amusement, blurred at Luna Park.

The production was lavishly staged throughout. Like the vaudeville palaces of the turn of the century and anticipating the ornate movie theaters of the 1920s, Luna appealed to popular notions of magnificence. Illusions of extravagance and ostentatious display provided a holiday compensation for the plainness and thrift required in everyday life. Elements such as the fantastic turreted façade of the "20,000 Leagues Under the Sea" exhibition and the elevated

(OPPOSITE, TOP) Luna Park, 1909; the Electric Tower

(OPPOSITE, BOTTOM) The "Dragon's Gorge," 1906; base of Electric Tower, 1908

65

promenade opposite, with its huge duck's-head decorations, lush plantings, and flags flying over all, were designed to fill visitors with a sense of importance. Thompson appropriated architectural symbols of luxury to confer upon his patrons an honored status. Before the mansions of the rich on New York's Fifth Avenue they might feel humbled and excluded, but here they could feel assured. Luna Park, in effect, democratized the hunger for aristocratic splendor that was driving rich industrialists to construct palatial houses at the turn of the century. It provided a Newport for the masses.[35]

Luna Park performed an additional transformation into a magical realm at night. Borrowing from the example of the White City, Thompson studded Luna with a quarter million electric lights. The same buildings that excited wonder during the day assumed a dazzling new aspect; the strings of lights seemed to sketch an insubstantial, dreamlike scene: "Tall towers that had grown dim suddenly broke forth in electric outlines and gay rosettes of color, as the living spark of light traveled hither and thither, until the place was transformed into an enchanted garden, of such a sort as Aladdin never dreamed."[36] The spectacle intensified visitors' sense of Coney as a magical realm that violated conventional rules. Luna turned night into day, a feat which symbolized its topsy-turvy order. Its buildings dramatically altered their appearance to achieve an even more festive air and invited visitors to do the same.

Behind Luna Park's architecture and its diverse attractions lay a broad but consistent rationale. As Frederic Thompson observed, visitors to the seaside resort "are not in a serious mood, and do not want to encounter seriousness. They have enough seriousness in their every-day lives, and the keynote of the thing they do demand is change. Everything must be different from ordinary experience. What is presented to them must have life, action, motion, sensation, surprise, shock, swiftness or else comedy." Thompson and his partner Dundy endeavored to satisfy these requirements, to create in Luna Park what Coney Island represented as a whole, "a different world— a dream world, perhaps a nightmare world—where all is bizarre and

ELEVATED PROMENADE, LUNA PARK, CONEY ISLAND, N.Y.

COPYRIGHT, 1904, BY A. LOEFFLER,
TOM

By the elevated
Promenade, Luna Park,
1904

fantastic—crazier than the craziest part of Paris—gayer and more different from the every-day world."[37]

In an effort to create this sense of a dream world filled with the "bizarre and fantastic," Thompson and Dundy assembled a profusion of exotic attractions in the tradition of the Chicago Midway. For its opening season Luna boasted a Venetian city complete with gondoliers, a Japanese garden, an Irish village, an Eskimo village, a Dutch windmill, and a Chinese theater. The following year, the park added a reproduction of the Durbar of Delhi and attempted to re-create its splendor. A newspaper reporter breathlessly described the scene: "There were gilded chariots and prancing horses, and trained elephants and dancing girls, regiments of soldiers, and an astonishing number of real Eastern people and animals in gay and stately trappings. The magnificence of the scene was such as to make those who witnessed it imagine they were in a genuine Oriental city."[38] In this way Luna appealed to visitors' imaginations, their hunger for the gorgeousness of foreign realms, their eagerness to taste splendors

Luna Park at night, 1904

(OPPOSITE) The Kaleidoscopic Tower, Luna Park, 1904

(LEFT) Riding the
elephant, Luna Park, 1905

(RIGHT) "King," the
diving horse

beyond their experience—but nonetheless on their terms. A ferry ride
to Coney thus became for middle- and working-class people a sub-
stitute for a steamship cruise abroad and Luna Park a Cook's tour in
miniature. While the resort served as an agent of Americanization
for immigrants and their children, Coney's amusements also indicated
a countervailing urge to venture beyond the confines of an assimila-
tionist culture, to rediscover the exotic, if only in the safe precincts
of what amounted to cultural zoos.

Indeed, Luna moved with notable ease from exotic architecture
and peoples to exotic animals, as Thompson and Dundy expanded
upon the formulas of earlier popular impresarios such as P. T. Barnum.[39] They boasted the largest herd of show elephants in the world,
and delighted in including them in special stunts, such as sliding
down a special Shoot-the-Chutes. For the "Streets of Delhi" they
offered a choice of elephants or camels for visitors to ride upon and
play the part of rajas. They installed a three-ring circus on raised
platforms over the lagoon at the foot of the Shoot-the-Chutes, featur-
ing equestrian acrobatics, a cakewalking pony, trained bears, and of
course more elephants. In their effort to provide gripping, thrilling

amusement, Luna's managers occasionally appealed to a latent cruelty in their audience in features such as "King," the diving horse, who leapt from a high platform into a tub of water, or, much more overtly, in the public and highly publicized execution of an old elephant, "Topsy," first by supposedly poisoned carrots, then, with undeniable authenticity, by electrocution.

Though this last instance was a rarity, the thrill of witnessing at least the illusion of death and destruction was routinely satisfied at Luna and elsewhere in Coney Island by various shows and displays. Showmen vied with one another in re-creating such famous disasters as "The Fall of Pompeii," simulating the eruption of Mount Vesuvius and the death of 40,000 people, the eruption of Mount Pelée and devastation of Martinique in 1902, Pennsylvania's Johnstown Flood of 1889, and Texas's Galveston Flood of 1900. For the first live disaster spectacle Luna chose a scene closer to home. In "Fire and Flames" a four-story building was repeatedly set ablaze, the fire

"Fire and Flames"

71

battled by heroic firemen while residents leaped from upper windows into safety nets below.

Such displays reflected a fascination with disaster in the late nineteenth and early twentieth centuries, a horrible delight in the apprehension that devastating tragedy had both historically and contemporaneously intruded suddenly in daily affairs, even in modern technological America.[40] In its very horror, disaster conferred a kind of transcendent meaning to its victims' lives, transforming commonplace routine into the extraordinary. Sensationalized re-creations of such disasters gave a vicarious sense of this transcendence to their audience—with of course the inestimable advantage of allowing them to emerge from the performance unharmed. Thus disasters have proved a staple of American popular art from Currier & Ives lithographs of steamboat explosions and flaming buildings in the mid-nineteenth century to *The Towering Inferno, The Poseidon Adventure, Earthquake,* and other films of the 1970s.

Luna leavened these ritual spectacles of disaster with broad comic farce. Like the "Barrel of Fun" in Steeplechase, various of Luna's devices were designed to amuse patrons by tricking them, by making their own foolish predicaments a part of the entertainment. As one journalist described the experience, "Within five minutes after your entrance to Luna you will try to tread on the trick walk, the planks of which, propelled by machinery from beneath, slide in all directions from under your feet. You will sit . . . in trick chairs, which, when your weight releases a hidden spring, tilt over and toss you away; or in benches that, by a similar device, collapse and double you up like your jackknife." Such devices gave pleasure by the way in which they violated conventional expectations and launched Luna's patrons into a world of the absurd. They invited people to view their world and themselves in their droll aspects, to accept and delight in the role of fools.[41] These contraptions mocked the world of productive devices by being intentionally counterproductive, systematically frustrating those who would expect them to fulfill their apparent functions.

(LEFT) Miners
descending for work

(RIGHT) Thrill seekers
descending for pleasure

Indeed, all of Coney Island's intricate machines and amusements were similarly unproductive, promising customers nothing more than the pleasure of the event itself; that was central to their character as play.[42] But the particular forms this play took were significant. In the effort to suggest a dream or nightmare world, Coney abstracted features from the larger society and presented them in intensified, fantastic forms. Instruments of production and efficiency were transformed into objects of amusement, and life around them lifted from dull routine to exhilarating pageantry.

This process is particularly striking in the case of the mechanized rides at Luna and elsewhere in Coney Island. These marked the culmination of a desire, evident throughout the nineteenth century and into the twentieth, not simply to view technology in utilitarian terms

73

but to value it as spectacle. Generations of Americans had thrilled in viewing huge steam engines, thundering locomotives, and other powerful machinery as sublime creatures harnessed to do their bidding. Mechanical amusement rides allowed them to cultivate the delight, awe, and fear of the technological sublime still more intensely. Some of Coney Island's rides, in fact, were directly inspired by modes of transportation in use in industry and society at large, beginning in 1884 with the Switchback Railroad, a forerunner of the roller coaster. The creator of the Switchback, LaMarcus Thompson, had discovered an abandoned coal mine where people eagerly paid to coast down the shafts in gravity-powered coal cars, and he saw the ride's potential in an amusement park. Thompson applied the idea straightforwardly in the Switchback, in which a car holding ten people coasted in a straight direction along a gently undulating track until the car came to a stop; then attendants pushed the car over a switch and up an incline to send them on a second set of tracks, parallel to the first, back to their starting point. Soon Thompson developed a mechanically assisted roller coaster which provided a scenic interlude—and, passengers joyfully discovered, romantic intimacy—by running the cars through a tunnel, as he continued to exploit the mining analogy.

Within a short time amusement entrepreneurs at Coney Island, Atlantic City, and similar resorts around the country were constructing elaborate and hair-raising roller coasters in attempts to outdo one another. These continued to borrow from the urban and industrial railways, so much so that some commentators marveled how much the amusements to which people flocked resembled the features of their daily life. As one journalist observed, "The switchbacks, scenic railways and toy trains are merely trolley cars, a little more uneven in roadbed, jerky in motion and cramped in the seat than the ordinary means of transportation, but not much."[43]

In fact, some rides seem perhaps intended as broad parodies of urban experiences. The "Flip-Flap" Railway at Sea Lion Park, where Luna Park was later erected, propelled daring twosomes rapidly down a track and through a twenty-five-foot vertical loop, thus apparently

(ABOVE) The El curve at 110th Street, 1898

(RIGHT) The "Flip-Flap" at Coney, 1900

defying the law of gravity and executing a dizzying mechanical somer-
sault. After such a ride, the worst twists of the New York Elevated
Railroad could hold no terror. Another Coney Island attraction, the
"Leap-Frog" Railway, thrilled passengers by sending two electric
cars, each filled with as many as forty people, toward one another
on the same set of tracks, heading for what appeared to be certain
collision. As the two cars neared and riders shuddered at the prospect

"Helter Skelter," Luna
Park, 1905

of their own disaster, one car glided along a set of curved rails up and over the roof of the other and continued serenely on its way.

Luna specialized in fanciful versions of these bracing rides, from simple gravity slides to complex mechanical contraptions. Some of these, as Frederic Thompson frankly asserted, were intended as "elaborated child's play."[44] For example, one ride devised by Thompson personally, the "Helter Skelter" or "Human Toboggan," was essentially a slide for adults. Participants rode an escalator to the top of a huge chute made of rattan, then rapidly coasted down its sinuous course, landing at the end on a mattress—all to the amusement of the onlooking crowd. Steeplechase Park developed its own version of this ride in the shape of a huge tobacco pipe, in which patrons entered at the mouthpiece and slid out the bowl.

The immensely popular water slide Shoot-the-Chutes worked on a similarly elementary principle. Passengers in flat-bottomed boats prepared to coast down a steep incline and across the lagoon as hundreds of spectators lined the rails to watch. "Ladies screamed,

Shooting the chutes,
Luna Park, 1903

children clung wildly to anybody within reach. One great shocking
plunge, a leap in the air, a heaving and a tossing, and the boat glided
into the waters of the lake, to be brought to a safe landing."[45] Groups
on a holiday held onto their hats and grinned with delight as they
leaned forward in the boats, exulting in the sense of transport and
posing to re-create it for the photographer.

Shooting the chutes . . .

. . . for the photographer

Frederic Thompson invented the "Mountain Torrent" as a more thrilling version of Shoot-the-Chutes. Here passengers embarked on a boat ride along a circuitous course down an inclined track by hills and waterfalls, through a tunnel and lake. Reportedly, the ride was "a most exciting one, and never fails to furnish material for wild screams."[46]

But visitors' desire to be whisked down inclines, spun, jolted, knocked off their feet would still not be satisfied. They thronged to Luna's "Witching Waves," devised, by the inventor of the revolving door, to simulate the bobbing of ships at sea, then perhaps to the "Whirl of the Wind" next to Luna's central tower, which offered a view of the park as a whole. They might then take one of several rides at Luna and elsewhere, such as the "Tickler," which featured spinning circular cars that moved down a winding pathway, in some versions caroming wildly into one another.

In various ways all these rides were designed to throw people off balance, literally and imaginatively, to sweep patrons up in their grasp and momentarily overwhelm them before allowing order to be restored at the end. Such rides served in effect as powerful hallucinogens, altering visitors' perceptions and transforming their consciousness, dispelling everyday concerns in the intense sensations of the

(LEFT) Preparing to ride the "Tickler," Luna Park, 1908

(RIGHT) Advertisement for "Loop the Loop," 1905

LOOP THE LOOP

The Greatest Sensation of the Age

THE SAFEST AND THE GREATEST ATTRACTION

NO DANGER WHATEVER

present moment. They allowed customers the exhilaration of whirl-wind activity without physical exertion, of thrilling drama without imaginative effort. Riders could enjoy their own momentary fright and disorientation because they knew it would turn to comic relief; they could engage in what appeared dangerous adventure because ultimately they believed in its safety. As advertisements for the "Loop the Loop," a variation of the "Flip-Flap," reassured customers: "The Greatest Sensation of the Age . . . No Danger Whatever."

The importance of sustaining the illusion of anarchic freedom and heedless release beneath the underlying reality of control under-lay all of Luna Park and Coney Island as a whole. The various rides were based upon the ability to coordinate mass activity through tech-nology, to assemble and disperse crowds at will without making such efforts oppressive. Similarly, amusement park managers assumed the task of promoting a sense of spontaneous gaiety through calculated means. Their success or failure, as Frederic Thompson insisted, de-pended upon their ability to cultivate by every device at their disposal an air of excitement and festivity, as he put it in a revealing phrase, to "manufacture the carnival spirit." Fantastic architecture, exotic attractions, swift and exhilarating rides, ballyhoos—all according to Thompson needed to be carefully designed to sweep people up in a festive mood and make the park a commercial success. Though he provided benches around Luna Park, Thompson hated to see cus-tomers sitting on them, for then in effect they were removing them-selves as actors in the spectacle and becoming a potentially detached and critical audience. When people sat down he would immediately dispatch a band of musicians to the scene in an attempt to rouse his customers' spirits and thus bring them to their feet.[47]

So phenomenal was Luna Park's success that within a year it stimu-lated another rival. A group of politicians headed by William H. Reynolds, a former New York state senator, theater manager, and well-known playboy, raised $3,500,000 to build Dreamland Park right across Surf Avenue from Luna. Dreamland took Luna's formula and expanded it. To overshadow Luna's massive gates, Dreamland

placed one of its chief attractions, "The Creation," immediately adjacent to the entrance; customers were enticed to the box office by a monumental female sculpture whose titillating nudity was supposedly excused by her religious character. Inside the gates Dreamland's architects aimed for an eclectic setting of lavish grandeur, dominated by a court of gleaming white buildings, columns, and statuary in a style that might be called Imperial Orgiastic. In an attempt to dwarf Luna's electrical tower, the designers of Dreamland erected a 375-foot central tower modeled on the Giralda in Seville. If the guidebooks are to be believed, the copy surpassed not only Luna but the Giralda itself; it was simply "the finest tower ever built."[48] To eclipse Luna's nighttime display, Dreamland installed a million electric lights, 100,000 for the tower alone.

The rivalry extended to specific attractions. Dreamland proudly announced not one but two Shoot-the-Chutes; its own disaster spectacles, including "Fighting the Flames," with a burning building two stories taller than Luna's and a cast of 4,000 characters; a Lilliputian village inhabited by 300 midgets; a simulated submarine and airplane ride, "Under and Over the Sea"; two scenic railways, "Coasting through Switzerland" and "The Great Divide"; a three-ring circus; and a dramatic animal show. Both Steeplechase and Luna had included ballrooms catering to the new craze for more sensual, intimate dancing—to the dismay of moralists ranging from conservative clergymen to the socialist *Jewish Daily Forward*. Once again Dreamland claimed to best its competitors with an immense Renaissance-style ballroom on Coney's old Iron Pier. With the rhetorical restraint characteristic of the business, the new amusement park was hailed as the "Gibraltar of the Amusement World."[49]

With the construction of Coney Island's three great amusement parks, the popular resort emerged as the unofficial capital of the new mass culture and aroused special interest among artists, writers, and critics. As various observers toured Coney Island and studied the multitudes, the experience stirred powerful responses. The resort raised profound questions in their minds about the nature of crowds, the ultimate influence of this new breed of amusement, and the future of American culture in an urban-industrial age.

Coney Island impressed observers first as spectacle, and its pictorial possibilities attracted a number of visual artists. A "vulgar" subject, Coney's amusement parks were anathema to genteel painters who still clung to approved "ideal" scenes of serene landscapes and stylish ladies of leisure. The popular resort's first depictors, therefore, were practitioners of what were regarded as "minor" arts: commercial photographers such as the Byron studio, Irving Underhill, Samuel H. Gottscho, Eugene Wemlinger, and the Detroit Photographic Company, whose works we have seen, accompanied occasionally by various illustrators. These photographers and sketchers acted as visual reporters. With a keen sense of the historic moment, they recognized in Coney profound cultural innovations. They intended their works not for museums but for mass-circulation magazines such as *Munsey's, Everybody's, Cosmopolitan,* and *Century,* which sought to inform and entertain a broad readership by presenting the colorful drama of the resort.

Soon these figures were joined by a new generation of painters, who were themselves searching for an alternative to the subject matter and spirit of their genteel academic predecessors. Whether realists or modernists, they turned to Coney Island for precisely the reasons more conservative painters spurned it. The amusement complex presented scenes which were stunningly technological, urban, populous, egalitarian, erotic, hedonistic, dynamic, and culturally diverse. For painters in revolt against decorous traditional standards, Coney Island offered in profusion the ingredients of a powerful new aesthetic.[50]

The response of the modernist Joseph Stella offers a striking case in point. Born in Italy, Stella had worked for several years in New York and Pittsburgh as a magazine illustrator before returning to Europe for further study. There he was exposed to both the Italian Futurist movement and French Cubism. When he arrived once again in New York in 1912 inspired by these influences, he saw afresh the artistic possibilities of the urban-industrial scene. He described himself "thrilled" with the spectacle of a new world of steel and electricity, surging with drama and demanding to be translated into a new art.[51]

Eager to capture this new world on canvas, Stella chose as his first subject the Mardi Gras carnival at Coney Island. This Mardi Gras was not a pre-Lenten holiday but a special post-Labor Day celebration which had been instituted, improbably enough, as a fundraising effort for the Coney Island Rescue Mission for wayward girls. Stella felt that he really needed a big wall to portray his subject adequately, but he contented himself with the largest canvas he could find. Then, as he described it, "I built the most intense dynamic arabesque that I could imagine in order to convey in a hectic mood the surging crowd and the revolving machines generating for the first time, not anguish and pain, but violent, dangerous pleasures."[52]

"Battle of Lights, Mardi Gras, Coney Island" (1913) is Stella's depiction of "the new bacchanal" that Coney Island embodied. In contrast to the approach of Coney Island photographers, who isolated and coolly recorded individual scenes, Stella amassed various elements to convey the total experience of the amusement complex. The painting suggests a barrage of sensations and emotions. The viewer is plunged into a dense and turbulent scene, a riot of swirling colors and shapes exploding in all directions. Multi-hued crowds surge upward from the bottom of the canvas toward the brilliant carnival to

Joseph Stella, "Battle of Lights, Mardi Gras, Coney Island"

89

Detail of "Battle of Lights"

be swept up and transformed by it. Above them dancing figures sway sensuously, outlined in pure vermilion, in Stella's words, "to accentuate the carnal frenzy." The spinning, tangled forms of the amusement rides, beckoning signs and searchlights dominate the upper half of the painting, capped by Luna Park's electric tower glowing like a bejeweled sultan's cap over the enchanted realm. On the far right a mask-like head observes the carnival—quite possibly a portrait of Stella himself in Harlequin dress.[53]

As Stella's title suggests, the painting is a battleground of contending forces, resulting in a dynamic synthesis. Warm and cool values clash explosively within the picture, and the paint is thickest at the center. Angular and curvilinear forms collide; mechanical and organic shapes swirl together. The effect is almost apocalyptic. Stella once referred to "Battle of Lights" as "the *Comedy* of Modern Machinery," but critics have correctly detected mixed emotions in his painting. The work conveys the essence of Coney Island's carnival in its exhilarating sense of release, of ecstatic disorientation, of dynamic activity and celebration. However, there exists as well a sense that the "carnal frenzy" and "violent, dangerous pleasures" may escape bounds. The hectic, propulsive rhythms allow no rest. The chaotic activity is almost suffocating in its profusion. As we shall see, Stella's powerfully ambivalent response to Coney Island was shared by numerous artists and critics.[54]

American realist painters of the early twentieth century only gradually discovered Coney Island, though ultimately they would passionately embrace it. More conventional than Stella in artistic style, these painters were nonetheless radical in subject matter. Some of the leading realists of the century's first decade—Robert Henri, John Sloan, George Luks, William Glackens, Everett Shinn—served their artistic apprenticeships as newspaper illustrators and thus learned firsthand the heterogeneous activity of the city ignored by genteel academicians. As artists they rebelled against the conservative canons of "tradition" and "refinement," celebrating instead the diversity of urban American life. Congregations of lower-middle- and working-class people appeared to them as vigorous expressions of the pageantry of the city, and scenes of amusement in public parks, saloons, poolrooms, vaudeville theaters, circuses, beaches, and amusement parks exerted a special fascination.

John Sloan epitomized their response to such subjects in a journal entry for July 13, 1907:

> Up rather late. A beautiful day so we think we will go out this afternoon. To Coney Island hie ourselves and have a very pleasant afternoon and evening. The concert halls with their tawdry, gaudy, bawdy beauties are fine—and on the beach, the sand covered bathing suits of the women who look and "cavort" are great—look like soft sandstone sculptures, full of the real "vulgar" human life. Crowds watch the people coming down the Bamboo slide in Luna Park—lingerie displays bring a roar of natural "vulgar" mirth. The crowds near kill you in the rushes for the trains going and coming. One must strive for good nature.[55]

Sloan delighted in the exuberant, unselfconscious vitality of the crowds, while regarding them with aesthetic detachment, social condescension, and a trace of uneasiness. Their very vigor might prove

Reginald Marsh,
"George C. Tilyou's
Steeplechase Park"

overwhelming, even dangerous. As he concluded, "One must strive
for good nature."

This fascination with the pictorial possibilities of urban amusement, cultivated by the realists of the decade 1900–10, blossomed
profusely in the work of their successors, especially the uncrowned
painter-laureate of Coney Island, Reginald Marsh. Beginning in the
early 1920s, Marsh visited Coney Island every summer, occasionally
three or four times a week. "On the first trip each summer," he
remarked, "I'm nauseated by the smell of stale food, but after that

I get so I don't notice it." Marsh strove to overcome his nausea as
Sloan strove for good nature because, like Stella and Sloan before
him, he was captivated by the spectacle of crowds swept up in the
carnival atmosphere, sprawling in dense pyramids on the beaches and
whirling voluptuously on amusement rides. In Coney Island he discovered a theater of experience which was the antithesis of his own
privileged background and genteel upbringing, and it held him
spellbound.[56]

To appreciate what Marsh found at Coney Island one need only
compare his picture "George C. Tilyou's Steeplechase Park" (1936)
with a turn-of-the-century photograph of the same scene. Marsh
enlarged his composition beyond the power of the photographer to
depict the "Human Whirlpool" in the foreground, the swinging
"Chair-o-plane" in the background, and throngs of spectators press-
ing against the rail at the center. On every level Marsh clustered his
subjects as thickly as possible and cast them in an orgy of casually
seductive postures. They do not merely stand and sit but lounge

The "Human Whirl-
pool" at Steeplechase
Park

and sprawl with arms pointing, legs spread, elbows and knees thrust every which way. The young women in the "Whirlpool" fairly explode out of their clothes in their sexual ripeness and availability. While fashions had grown more informal since the turn of the century, Marsh did not depict changes from the earlier time so much as he made the eroticism of Coney Island explicit in a way the photographer could not. Both photograph and picture concern the pleasure of witnessing pleasure, as we view the spectators who view the riders. (In the photograph, to complete the process, the spectators look back at us.) But while the photographer focused upon the whirling motion of the wheel, Marsh delighted most in the fleshy character of the scene. His works summarize the perspective of an earlier generation of artists and intellectuals who observed with ambivalent fascination the vulgarity and beauty, sordidness and eroticism, spontaneity and commercialism of America's emergent mass culture.

The pleasure-seeking crowds portrayed by Stella and later Marsh also attracted a number of journalists and cultural critics who came to observe the Feast of Fools for themselves. They too were immediately struck by the spirit of release—some would have said of license. As Richard Le Gallienne put it, "Coney Island is the Tom-Tom of America. Every nation has, and needs—and loves—its Tom-Tom. It has its needs of orgiastic escape from respectability—that is, from the world of What-we-have-to-do into the world of What-we-would-like-to-do, from the world of duty that endureth forever into the world of joy that is graciously permitted for a moment." The spirit of carnival and the shedding of workday roles and respectability was infectious, well-nigh irresistible. Again and again writers described how customarily staid and dignified figures—themselves included!—were swept up in the carnival and plunged into the strenuous merrymaking, sloughing off their critical detachment and propriety. "To slip dimes and quarters through silly ticket windows, to swelter in stuffy amusement pens, to cancel every canon of conventionality, every rubric of discretion, to court perils, discomforts, and mellow swindles—such is your symphony. You spy on your soul and laughingly exclaim, 'Lawkamassy on us, this is none of I.' "[57]

Yet even while critics themselves responded to the carnival spirit, they often scrutinized the crowds about them carefully. Coney Island offered a case study in collective behavior for observers to ponder, one which many regarded as a significant harbinger of the emergent American culture. Some returned with reassuring messages for their readership. In contrast to the unsavory Coney Island of the McKane era, the crowds appeared orderly and thoroughly decent in their merrymaking. "It is the ordinary American crowd," concluded one reporter, "the best natured, best dressed, best behaving and best smelling crowd in the world; not vulgar unless we mean by that, as many do, being obviously and audibly amused . . ."[58] Coney Island, these observers appeared to suggest with sighs of relief, did not mark any basic departure from the traditional values of American middle-class culture.

However, a few critics, more openly critical of the genteel tradition, insisted that Coney Island did indeed signal a cultural innovation and a welcome one at that. In their judgment the spirit of carnival appeared to be leavening native American seriousness with a sense of joyfulness. They applauded Coney Island as a crucible of democratic freedom and equality, a cultural melting pot mingling individuals and races from all segments of society. If this emergent culture was crude in some respects, it was irresistibly genial. As one journalist wrote, "he must be a hardened aristocrat or a bigoted esthete who can resist [Coney's] spirit of enjoyment or refuse to respond to its frank assumption of equality . . . Bare human nature, naïve and unashamed, stands up at Coney and cries out 'Brother' and the unanimity with which human nature responds is hopeful though disconcerting."[59]

Nonetheless, the unrepressed new culture of Coney Island deeply troubled other observers—not all of whom were "hardened aristocrats or bigoted esthetes." The spectacle of "bare human nature" crying out "Brother" repelled them more than it pleased; they heartily wished he would check his fraternal affections and get dressed. The

James Gibbons Huneker

response of James Gibbons Huneker is especially interesting in this respect. An enthusiastic and iconoclastic critic, Huneker ranged freely over music, literature, art, and other subjects from the 1890s to the 1920s, often in vigorous defense of artistic novelty. But when he ventured to Coney Island in the 1910s to see this new cultural institution and aesthetic in action, most of what he saw moved him to despair. He denounced the whole complex as "a disgrace to our civilisation" and urged its immediate abolition. Not that he didn't enjoy himself, he admitted, "for when you are at Coney you cast aside your hampering reason and become a plain lunatic."[60]

What disturbed Huneker, in fact, was precisely the surrender of reason, even of repression, that Coney encouraged. "After the species of straitjacket that we wear in every-day life is removed at such Saturnalia as Coney Island," he observed dryly, "the human animal emerges in a not precisely winning guise." From this perspective, Coney's topsy-turvy entertainments and fantastic architecture were not harmless pleasures but evidences of cultural delirium: "Unreality is as greedily craved by the mob as alcohol by the dipsomaniac; indeed, the jumbled nightmares of a morphine eater are actually realised at Luna Park." Other visitors might be impressed by the orderliness and friendliness of the crowd; Huneker feared its susceptibility to manipulation and excess. In the disorienting whirl of collective activity he sensed not the spirit of democracy fulfilled but of primitivism unleashed. "Once en masse," Huneker warned darkly, "humanity sheds its civilisation and becomes half child, half savage. . . . It will lynch an innocent man or glorify a scamp politician with equal facility. Hence the monstrous debauch of the fancy at Coney Island, where New York chases its chimera of pleasure." From barbaric entertainment he saw emerging a barbaric new culture.[61]

In articulating these opinions, Huneker was not merely voicing idiosyncratic fears, but expressing concerns frequently advanced by leading behavioral scientists of the period. According to the dominant school of American psychiatry in the late nineteenth and early twentieth centuries, the genteel virtues of sobriety, diligence, thrift, and self-mastery safeguarded not only family and society but sanity itself. By encouraging sensuous self-abandon, then, Coney Island in a very real sense promoted lunacy. In addition, beginning in the 1890s a number of influential social psychologists, both European and American, focused on crowds as a topic for special study. In the works of these scholars, the presence of the crowd brought a lessening of customary restraints and an explosion of repressed impulses. According to one of the most illustrious American sociologists, Edward A. Ross, the "crowd self" was "ephemeral," "unstable," "credulous," "irrational," and "immoral." Reason was paralyzed in the crowd, emotion intensified: "Masked by their anonymity, people feel free to give rein to the expression of their feelings. To be heard, one does not speak; one shouts. To be seen, one does not simply show one's self; one gesticulates. Boisterous laughter, frenzied objurgations, frantic cheers, are needed to impress the merriment or wrath or enthusiasm of the crowd."[62] Such theories cast the exaggerated behavior of Coney Island in a most disturbing light. The spectacle of masses of people anonymously congregating to participate in intensely emotional amusements seemed like social dynamite. With frightening ease a peaceful group of pleasure seekers like those George Bellows painted in "Beach at Coney Island" (1908–10) might erupt into a demonic mob, like the spectators in his contemporary painting "Both Members of This Club" (1909).

If the propensity of the crowd was inherently primitive, some observers believed this tendency was exacerbated by the growing proportion of immigrants from Southern and Eastern Europe. Shuddering at the vulgar multitude of Coney even as he sought it out, Huneker fondly recalled the day when New York had not yet become "the dumping-ground of the cosmos." By 1921 *The New Republic*'s Bruce Bliven would complain that the hair on most heads along Coney Island's beach was black. Here as elsewhere, Bliven announced with disgust, a new population was displacing "native American stock," and "Anglo-Saxon Puritanism," which had historically formed "the framework of American manners," was forced to yield before displays of "love-making on the beach." Established traditions, rules of conduct, values, all appeared to be crumbling under the onslaught of a mongrel mass culture.[63]

Bliven, it is important to note, wrote not as a carping aristocrat but as one of a large number of progressive intellectuals and reformers in the early twentieth century concerned with the character of American recreation, for Coney Island raised issues that were central to progressive reform. Coney held up a mirror to the larger society—albeit the grotesque distorting mirror of a fun house—and reflected a general crisis in American culture. Progressive reformers repeatedly lamented the fact that modern American cities were organized only in the service of work and profit; no provision had been made for the organization of community life and leisure. As a result, they believed, society had become dangerously unbalanced. The social restraints that had traditionally prevailed in small towns had collapsed in modern cities with nothing to take their place. Face-to-face communities provided important checks on behavior; by contrast, the anonymous life of the metropolis appeared to leave individuals rootless and unrestrained. The intricate network of family and kinship ties, of social supervision and group life that working-class people developed within the city, defied the categories of these reformers and characteristically escaped their notice. With few exceptions they saw in the culture of the urban working class not creative adaptation but pathological disintegration.

Not only the pressures but even the very abundance of the industrial economy posed problems for the maintenance of traditional social controls. At the very time Coney Island's amusement parks were attracting greatest attention, the economist and social theorist Simon Patten announced a "new basis of civilization." Industrial society, he contended, had moved from a "pain economy," where the scarcity of resources demanded a struggle for subsistence, to a "pleasure economy," in which abundance was potentially available to all. In making this declaration, Patten saw reason for concern as well as celebration. Scarcity had constituted the basic support of traditional

(OPPOSITE, TOP)
George Bellows, "Beach at Coney Island"

(OPPOSITE, BOTTOM)
George Bellows, "Both Members of This Club"

98

National Gallery of Art, Washington, D.C., Gift of Chester Dale

moral prohibitions. People avoided the sins of intemperance for fear of misery. In an age of abundance, what restraints were to be put in scarcity's place? What would protect society from debauch?[64]

Adding to these concerns, at the time Patten wrote a number of social critics feared the demands of industrial work invited debauchery. As the liberal cleric and reformer Walter Rauschenbusch observed, "The long hours and the high speed and pressure of industry use up the vitality of all except the most capable. An exhausted body craves rest, change, and stimulus, but it responds only to strong and coarse stimulation."[65] From the fatigue of modern work and the frustrations of urban industrial life in general individuals demanded relief. In the absence of wholesome public recreation, they turned to commercialized forms, dance halls, music halls, cheap theaters, brothels, saloons, and amusement parks like Coney Island.

Such entertainments, reformers contended, provided escape rather than renewal. As Jane Addams warned, " 'Looping the loop' amid shrieks of stimulated terror or dancing in disorderly saloon halls, are perhaps the natural reactions to a day spent in noisy factories and in trolley cars whirling through the distracting streets, but the city which permits them to be the acme of pleasure and recreation to its young people, commits a grievous mistake." Some urban reformers sharing Addams's convictions itched to tear down Coney Island's cheap commercial entertainments and to convert the site to a public park. In the tradition of F. L. Olmsted, they urged pastoral nostrums for urban ills. Nonetheless, Coney Island's critics grudgingly acknowledged that despite the oceanside setting, features of physical beauty hardly accounted for the resort's immense popularity. They marveled at the irony of "vast hordes of people rushing to the oceanside, to escape the city's din and crowds and nervous strain, and, once within sight and sound of the waves, courting worse din, denser crowds, and an infinitely more devastating nervous strain inside an inclosure whence the ocean cannot possibly be seen." From this vantage point, the very popularity of Coney Island testified to the double debasement of American culture—in both work and play environments. It represented, in the phrase of one writer, "an artificial distraction for an artificial life."[66]

For progressive reformers, then, attractions such as Coney Island were essentially frauds, perversions of play. Special interests, they charged, had discovered "the natural resource of the play instinct and [were] exploiting it for gain as they have exploited other great natural resources." In their cynical pursuit of gain, amusement promoters resorted to sensational appeals. They worked up the "carnival spirit" for maximum financial profit. Unsophisticated customers, caught up in the spirit of revelry of the crowd, surrendered not only their money but in many cases their virtue as well: "the innocent under multiplied and insistent suggestions can be reduced into intoxication and immorality in the space of a few hours, and the whole gamut of illicit relations foisted on them."[67]

Such criticisms, of course, were not limited to amusement parks. Reformers voiced similar critiques against many of the recreations of the new mass culture. Amusement parks, melodrama theaters, movie houses, dance halls, and similar institutions were all distrusted not only because of their commercial ends but also because of what middle-class authorities perceived as the regressive character of their activities. All of these entertainments depended on a lessened self-possession, a surrender of intellect and emotions to powerfully influential forces under the control of those who promised only pleasure and pursued only profit. (Later critics would denounce rock concerts with their hallucinatory power—and hallucinogenic drugs—in similar terms.) Middle-class moral guardians felt themselves to be losing control over the activities and values of the lower classes and even over their own young, and they moved to monitor the new entertainment centers as part of a struggle to regain their cultural authority.[68]

To restore the purity of play, to rescue this vital natural resource from commercial despoilers, reformers advocated a characteristic progressive solution: government regulation and expert supervision. Under enlightened municipal auspices, recreation could serve as a powerfully constructive force in social integration and moral develop-

Undisciplined play in
the street

ment. In the vision of progressive reformers community pageants, such as "safe and sane" Fourth of July celebrations, would rekindle a sense of common purpose and democratic faith. Public parks and gymnasiums would replace city streets as the playgrounds of the poor and, by instilling habits of discipline and cooperation, help to eradicate poverty itself. Community centers would supplant poolrooms and saloons as agents in the acculturation of recent immigrants. Recreation programs for factory workers and their families would make employees more content and productive. In such ways, reformers wished to supersede amusement parks and other commercial recreations with more orderly and highly regulated amusements, designed to discipline instincts and institutionalize them.

Although proponents of the "play movement," as it was called,

wished to include people of all ages, they concentrated particularly
on the role of play in the development of the young. In their eyes, the
play-forms of childhood were the building blocks of a culture, upon
which the future of American ideals depended. Hence the conduct of
play was a matter of utmost importance. In devising programs for
youth, recreational reformers came to advocate not "free" but "directed" play, with orderly activities, correlated schedules, and a clear
sense of the lessons to be taught by each activity. From childhood
to adulthood, the approved progression was from imitative play
through competitive play to cooperative play. As a leading figure in
the play movement, Luther H. Gulick, wrote:

> The sandpile for the small child, the playground for the
> middle-sized child, the athletic field for the boy, folk-dancing

103

and social ceremonial life for the boy and girl in the teens, wholesome means of social relationships during these periods, are fundamental conditions without which democracy cannot continue, because upon them rests the development of that self-control which is related to an appreciation of the needs of the rest of the group and of the corporate conscience, which is rendered necessary by the complex interdependence of modern life.[69]

"Self-control." "Corporate conscience." These were the civic qualities reformers saw proper play teaching, qualities they deemed essential in an urban-industrial democracy. Disciplined, structured play would achieve self-control rather than the self-abandon that so disturbed many observers at Coney Island, corporate conscience rather than mob license. The contrasting kinds of play, to the minds of a number of reformers, meant the difference between a community and a crowd, perhaps even the difference between civilization and barbarism.

Yet here again, as so often among middle-class observers, Coney Island stirred in reformers a complex response. It aroused an ambivalence that went to the heart of progressive reform. Progressive thinkers characteristically stressed the malleability of human attitudes and behavior. The social environment in which individuals matured and functioned decisively shaped their lives for good or ill. Truly effective reform, therefore, could not proceed on a piecemeal basis; it demanded the restructuring of the entire social order. Thus the scope of progressive reform extended far beyond the political and economic spheres to include every aspect of American life. Society as a whole was an educational institution and one which cried out for curricular reform.

Because of progressives' interest in reform of the social environment as a whole, Coney Island exerted a special fascination. For Coney in its own way represented, as one amusement park manager had boasted, a vast laboratory of human behavior, a demonstration—disturbing to many—of precisely how malleable human beings were. At a time when many progressives were interested in the possibilities of social engineering and social control through the construction of healthful environments for collective action, the example of Coney Island was especially galling because here entrepreneurs engineered society for what reformers adjudged decidedly unprogressive ends. In their horror of Coney Island was a disguised admiration. As one social scientist expressed it, the "Devil appears to be the only sociologist who, in modern times, has given his mind to the subject" of recreation.[70]

Pondering how to institute progressive social controls, the social theorist Simon Patten was prepared not only to give the devil his due but to learn from his methods. He noted approvingly how Coney Island and other commercial recreations served as important instruments of socialization, especially in converting the "stragglers of industry . . . into the steady ranks of disciplined workers." Young employees' "zest for amusement," Patten observed, "urges them to submit to the discipline of work, and the habits formed for the sake of gratifying their tastes make their regular life necessary in industry easier and more pleasant." He urged educators and philanthropists to heed the lessons to be derived from such amusements, that people inevitably sought pleasure and by that desire could be adjusted to their roles in the industrial world. The "craving to be amused," hitherto exploited for private gain, could in fact serve as the basis for a more efficient and cohesive social order. The carrot of amusement, "attractive social control," in Patten's view was far more effective than the stick of more restrictive measures.[71] Such statements expose the underlying links between Coney Island entrepreneurs and progressive reformers. Both wished to manipulate the responses of the multitude—one in the service of social progress, the other in the service of profit.

For Coney Island was necessarily an imperfect Feast of Fools, an institutionalized bacchanal. It represented a festival that did not express joy *about* something, but offered "fun" in a managed celebration for commercial ends. Dispensing standardized amusement, it demanded standardized responses. Beneath the air of liberation, its pressures were profoundly conformist, its means fundamentally manipulative.

While encouraging the revelry of the crowd, Coney Island's managers aimed always to shape and control it. Not only did they have to winnow out undesirables; they also needed to engineer the environment so as to keep customers in the role of active consumers. Amusement parks thus pioneered merchandising techniques that designers of shopping malls would later adopt: dramatizing objects of desire, elevating goods and attractions to fetishes, they made spending a pageant.

As the cultural upheaval of the early twentieth century has solidified, these characteristics of amusement parks have grown increasingly pronounced. Offended by the tawdriness of amusement parks such as Coney Island, Walt Disney sanitized them for the solidly middle class. California's Disneyland, Florida's Disney World, and the myriad "theme" parks that dot the country have perfected the administration of amusement in a way at which Tilyou and Thompson would have marveled. In the process these new parks have also stripped amusement of the vulgar exuberance that gave Coney Island its vitality. With the genteel culture no longer a real opponent, the elements of farce, clowning, and nonsense have given way to the canned reverence and robotized responses of Disney's "Hall of the Presidents." Sexual symbolism has been supplanted by technological perfectionism; urban heterogeneity has yielded to the clean-cut corporate homogeneity of "the American way."

What, then, was ultimately the function of Coney Island and the type of amusement it represented? If the popular resort appeared to symbolize revolt from genteel cultural standards, in what direction did this revolt lead? While Coney Island indeed helped to displace genteel culture with a new mass culture, this was not the subversive development conservative critics feared. Rather it represented a cultural accommodation to the developing urban-industrial society in a tighter integration of work and leisure than ever before.

At the turn of the century the nation was beginning a pivotal transition from an economy organized around production to one organized around consumption and leisure as well. Many of the values preached by genteel reformers and propagated by capitalist employers in the nineteenth century—hard work, punctuality, thrift, sobriety, self-control—were geared to the need for productivity. However, as the mass production of commodities created increasing abundance, it required an expanded mass market to absorb them. The period of Coney Island's heyday before the First World War saw the beginnings of the effort to develop that market and the increased application of technology to leisure-time pursuits. Phenomena as apparently diverse as mail-order catalogues, Model T Fords, movie serials, and mechanized amusement rides all were designed to enlarge merchandisers' and entertainers' clientele by selling to the vast multitude and amusing the million.

In this changed social setting, the old genteel injunctions lost their force. The rewards promised for those who conformed to such strictures—upward mobility, family security, social respectability—grew less compelling as new agencies emerged that offered far more immediate gratification. Coney Island and other popular amusements prospered not by promising the attainment of ultimate rewards but by providing instant pleasures and momentary release from work demands and social prescriptions.

With the 1920s this new economy and culture of consumption would expand enormously, although its salient characteristics had already been determined. Mass production, mass distribution, and installment buying allowed people of moderate means to acquire products similar to those of the rich, from automobiles to electric ranges and toasters. The advertising industry took as its mission the stimulation of consumption and the creation of new wants by quickening public appetite for alluring accouterments of the Good Life. As movies and radio swelled into major entertainment industries, they reinforced these consumer values and aspirations. The mass culture which had first emerged in the cities was now disseminated nationwide. The result was to endow a new middle-class ideal of consumption with as much if not more authority than the genteel culture had ever been able to command.[72]

To what degree Coney Island and the new mass culture it represented marked an increase in freedom obviously depends upon one's perspective. For many middle-class writers, Coney represented a loss of deference to older genteel standards, a vulgar and disorderly pursuit of sensation rather than the cultivation of sensibility they stood for. The result, to their minds, was a dangerous loss of social controls, an increase not of freedom but of license. However, for Coney's lower-middle- and working-class visitors and particularly for the foreign-born and their children, the amusement parks and the emergent mass culture offered an opportunity to participate in American life on a new basis, outside traditional forms and proscriptions. Though class divisions clearly remained, the success of the commercial mass culture depended on its ability to be inclusive rather than exclusive, to encourage a sense of access on a variety of levels.

From a third perspective, nonetheless, Coney Island and the new mass culture generally signified not liberation but a new form of subjection. Various critics and reformers raised this issue when they noted how visitors to Coney sought escape from the demands of urban-industrial life, yet were so totally creatures of their environment that they turned for recreation to a fantastic replication of that life. Amusement thus became an extension of work; a mechanized, standardized character pervaded both experiences. To counteract weariness and boredom, Coney Island prescribed a homeopathic remedy of intense, frenetic physical activity without imaginative demands.[73]

Maxim Gorky

The visitor who most fully perceived this aspect of Coney Island was not an American at all, but the Russian writer and revolutionary Maxim Gorky, who visited the resort in 1906. Viewing the amusement complex at night from a distance, Gorky responded enthusiastically to its promise. But as he scrutinized the resort and its visitors more closely, he was dismayed to discover not joy or transport but a "contented *ennui*." Entertainers and customers alike appeared to be wearily going through the motions of amusement, quickening their interest only at the prospect of cruelty or danger. The whole scene Gorky pronounced a "marsh of glittering boredom," particularly pernicious because it stupefied the working people, poisoned their souls, and reinforced their subjection. Concluded Gorky, "Life is made for the people to work six days in the week, sin on the seventh, and pay for their sins, confess their sins, and pay for the confession." In an age of mass culture, amusement emerged as the new opiate of the people.[74]

Gorky's view was an extreme one, which the editor of the American magazine that printed it suggested revealed more about Gorky than his subject.[75] Yet while Gorky minimized the pleasures Coney Island provided, he raised forcefully if crudely the point other critics had only suggested: Coney Island did not lead to true cultural revolt, but served to affirm the existing culture. Rather than suggesting alternatives to the prevailing economic and social order, as carnivals have often done in other cultures, Coney acted as a safety valve, a mechanism of social release and control that ultimately protected existing society. Its fantasy led not to a new apprehension of social possibilities, but toward passive acceptance of the cycle of production and consumption. The egalitarian spirit it fostered paradoxically served to reconcile visitors to the inequalities of society at large.[76]

The difficulty Coney Island's entrepreneurs faced was to continue to offer pleasure without effort on the part of consumers while keeping the experience from hardening into conscious boredom. The owners and managers of the three great amusement parks were well aware of this need and sought to meet it as best they could. While "manufacturing the carnival spirit," in Frederic Thompson's phrase, they aimed to give their products at least a superficial variety. The success of their entire venture depended upon maintaining the appearance of freshness, in sustaining the sense of contrast between Coney Island and society at large. "Novelty, that's the answer," insisted Samuel Gumpertz, the manager of Dreamland. "None of these park amusements is lasting. Few people try one more than half a dozen times in a visit and almost nobody wants the same thing the next season. The only way to make an old show go is to hang out a new sign— and that won't work more than one time with the audience."[77]

Awareness of the problem, however, did not necessarily yield a

solution. As the least innovative of the three parks, Dreamland in particular ran into financial difficulties almost from the beginning. Then in 1911 the amusement park unwittingly staged a disaster spectacle of unprecedented proportions as fire broke out in a ride appropriately called "Hell Gate" and spread with terrible swiftness throughout Dreamland, burning it to the ground. The elaborate amusement park was never rebuilt; instead manager Gumpertz devoted his energies to the far less ambitious Dreamland Circus Sideshow, a motley array of curiosities and freaks, both genuine and fraudulent. With the clarity of hindsight and perhaps a touch of sour grapes, one of Dreamland's directors blamed the park's difficulties on the debased taste of the public: "The promoters of Dreamland sought to appeal to a highly developed sense of the artistic," he declared solemnly, "but it did not take them long to discover that Coney Island was scarcely the place for that sort of thing. Architectural and decorative beauty were virtually lost upon the great majority of visitors, with the result that from year to year Dreamland was popularized, that is to say, the original design abandoned."[78]

Coney Island. N.Y. 1911

Less dramatically than Dreamland, Luna Park also fell into
decline. The partner in charge of finances, Skip Dundy, died suddenly
in 1907, while still in his mid-forties. Without Dundy's guidance,
Thompson soon foundered on a shoal of professional and personal
difficulties. By 1912 his marriage had failed and his alcoholism had
grown chronic. In that year Thompson declared bankruptcy. Thereafter, he worked at Luna as manager rather than owner until his
death in 1919 at the age of forty-six. Without the leadership of
showmen like Dundy and Thompson, Luna lost its innovative character and wore the old formulas threadbare to declining revenues.
Finally, in what has been called "merciful euthanasia," Luna in its
turn succumbed to a series of fires in the 1940s, to be replaced by a
parking lot and later a housing development.[79]

Thus, Steeplechase, the first of Coney's three great amusement
parks, was also the last, surviving in reduced form to the present
day.[80] Steeplechase also suffered fires, including a disastrous blaze as
early as 1907. With the resiliency of a pioneer, however, George
Tilyou immediately posted a sign promising "a bigger, better, Steeple-

111

chase Park," adding: "Admission to the Burning Ruins—10 cents." When Tilyou died in 1914, his son Edward and other members of the family managed it in his stead. But by the 1920s the younger Tilyou found it necessary to take increasingly forceful measures to keep customers entertained and to ward off boredom. Addressing his public, he declared frankly, "You respond instantly to incandescent cupolas, the blare of music, the slam of scenic railways, the beating of tom-toms; and we give you what you want. . . . The tenseness of modern industry and business competition has keyed your nervous organism to such a pitch that you seek a sharp stimulus."[81]

The problem Coney Island entrepreneurs faced by the 1920s was that the rest of the culture was catching up. The authority of the older genteel order that the amusement capital had challenged was now crumbling rapidly, and opportunities for mass entertainment were more abundant than ever. A long-time Coney Island resident would later observe, "Once upon a time Coney Island was the greatest amusement resort in the world. The radio and the movies killed it. The movies killed illusions."[82] More accurately, radio and movies made amusement ubiquitous, and the movies in particular presented elaborate, convincing illusions at a price Coney Island could not match. From great amusement park spectaculars, Coney came to rely more and more on the sideshows that had been its stock-in-trade before Steeplechase, Luna, and Dreamland were built. It was not that attendance at Coney declined in the 1920s—on the contrary, it increased—but the experience was less extraordinary and hence less meaningful. The extension of the subway from New York to Coney Island in 1920 made the resort more accessible than ever before, but it also reduced the element of contrast, the distinctive sense of entering a special realm operating under its own laws. The experience of the city and the experience of the resort increasingly blurred. Coney declined most markedly in the power to astound, and cultural critics stopped paying attention. A harbinger of the new mass culture, Coney Island lost its distinctiveness by the very triumph of its values.

1. On American genteel culture, see Daniel Walker Howe, "American Victorianism as a Culture," *American Quarterly,* 27 (December 1975): 507–32; and Stow Persons, *The Decline of American Gentility* (New York: Columbia University Press, 1973).

2. The revolt of intellectuals against the genteel middle class is brilliantly discussed in Christopher Lasch, *The New Radicalism in America* (New York: Knopf, 1965).

3. See John Higham, "The Reorientation of American Culture in the 1890's," in *Writing American History* (Bloomington: Indiana University Press, 1970), pp. 73–102.

4. Albert Fein, *Frederick Law Olmsted and the American Environmental Tradition* (New York: Braziller, 1972), pp. 23, 8; Olmsted, "Public Parks and the Enlargement of Towns," in *Civilizing American Cities: A Selection of Frederick Law Olmsted's Writings on City Landscapes,* ed. S. B. Sutton (Cambridge, Mass.: M.I.T. Press, 1971), pp. 65–66.

5. Geoffrey Blodgett, "Frederick Law Olmsted: Landscape Architecture as Conservative Reform," *Journal of American History,* 62 (March 1976): 881; Henry W. Bellows, "Cities and Parks: With Special Reference to the New York Central Park," *Atlantic Monthly,* 7 (April 1861): 428–29; Frederick Law Olmsted, Jr., and Theodora Kimball, eds., *Frederick Law Olmsted: Landscape Architect, 1822–1903* (New York: Putnam's, 1928), 2: 171.

6. Olmsted and Kimball, *Olmsted,* 2: 95–97, 109.

7. David F. Burg, *Chicago's White City of 1893* (Lexington: University Press of Kentucky, 1976), p. 77. On the Columbian Exposition as an expression of a cultural elite, see, in addition to Burg, John G. Cawelti, "America on Display: The World's Fairs of 1876, 1893, 1933," in *The Age of Industrialism in America,* ed. Frederic Cople Jaher (New York: Free Press, 1968), pp. 317–63; and Helen Lefkowitz Horowitz, *Culture and the City: Cultural Philanthropy in Chicago from the 1880s to 1917* (Lexington: University Press of Kentucky, 1976).

8. Saint-Gaudens is quoted in Cawelti, "America on Display," p. 338. On the Renaissance as a cultural ideal, see Horowitz, *Culture and the City,* pp. 19–20, 86–90.

9. Lloyd to Burnham, 26 March 1895, quoted in Thomas S. Hines, *Burnham of Chicago: Architect and Planner* (New York: Oxford University Press, 1974), p. 120; Henry Adams, *The Education of Henry Adams* (Boston: Houghton Mifflin, 1918), p. 343; William Dean Howells, "Letters of an Altrurian Traveller," *Cosmopolitan,* 16 (December 1893): 219. For other responses to the Exposition, see Burg, *Chicago's White City,* chap. 7.

10. Hamlin Garland, *A Son of the Middle Border* (New York: Macmillan, 1917), pp. 458–61.

11. Olmsted to Burnham, 20 June 1893, Olmsted Papers, Library of Congress, Washington, D.C.

12. Horowitz, *Culture and the City,* pp. 74–82.

13. *Portrait Types of the Midway Plaisance* (St. Louis: N. D. Thompson Pub-

lishing Co., 1893), n.p.; J[ames] W. Buel, *The Magic City* (St. Louis: Historical Publishing Co., 1894), n.p.

14. For material on the history of Coney Island throughout this book, I have drawn upon Eugene L. Armbruster, *Coney Island* (New York: privately printed, 1924); Oliver Pilat and Jo Ranson, *Sodom by the Sea: An Affectionate History of Coney Island* (Garden City, N.Y.: Doubleday, Doran & Co., 1941); Edo McCullough, *Good Old Coney Island* (New York: Scribner's, 1957); Lucy P. Gillman, "Coney Island," *New York History*, 36 (July 1955): 255–90; William F. Mangels, *The Outdoor Amusement Industry* (New York: Vantage Press, 1952); Gary Kyriazi, *The Great American Amusement Parks* (Secaucus, N.J.: Citadel Press, 1976), chaps. 2–3; and Robert E. Snow and David E. Wright, "Coney Island: A Case Study in Popular Culture and Technical Change," *Journal of Popular Culture*, 9 (Spring 1976): 960–75. Charles E. Funnell provides a thoughtful analysis of a related resort in *By the Beautiful Sea: The Rise and High Times of That Great American Resort, Atlantic City* (New York: Knopf, 1975).

15. Quotation from [Joel Cook], *Coney Island* (New York: Iron Steamboat Company, 1883), p. 19.

16. Edwin E. Slosson, "The Amusement Business," *Independent*, 57 (21 July 1904): 134.

17. Frederic Thompson, "Amusing the Million," *Everybody's Magazine*, 19 (September 1908): 378.

18. Slosson, "Amusement Business," p. 139; Lindsay Denison, "The Biggest Playground in the World," *Munsey's Magazine*, 33 (August 1905): 564–65. The social surveys are Louise Bolard More, *Wage-Earners' Budgets* (New York: H. Holt and Co., 1907), p. 142; and Robert Coit Chapin, *The Standard of Living Among Workingmen's Families in New York City* (New York: Russell Sage Foundation, 1909), pp. 211, 276.

19. Ruth S. True, *The Neglected Girl*, Russell Sage Foundation West Side Studies Series (New York: Survey Associates, 1914), pp. 59–60, 69–70; Belle Lindner Israels, "The Way of the Girl," *Survey*, 22 (3 July 1909): 487–88.

20. Ira Rosenwaike, *Population History of New York City* (Syracuse: Syracuse University Press, 1972), pp. 71, 88–89, 95–96.

21. Collection of Coney Island postcards at the Long Island Historical Society.

22. Guy Wetmore Carryl, "Marvelous Coney Island," *Munsey's Magazine*, 25 (September 1901): 814. In my interpretation of Coney Island as a special kind of social situation, I have been influenced by Erving Goffman's richly suggestive book, *Behavior in Public Places* (New York: Free Press, 1963); and also by the concept of liminality developed by Victor Turner in *The Ritual Process* (Chicago: Aldine, 1969); and *Dramas, Fields and Metaphors* (Ithaca: Cornell University Press, 1974), pp. 13–14, 52–53, 231–32.

23. Samuel Chotzinoff, *A Lost Paradise* (New York: Knopf, 1955), p. 81.

24. Pilat and Ranson, *Sodom*, p. 214; McCullough, *Coney Island*, p. 310; see James R. McGovern, "The American Woman's Pre-World War I Freedom in Manners and Morals," *Journal of American History*, 55 (September 1968): 315–33.

25. "Current Comment," *Illustrated American Magazine,* 12 (20 August 1892):
7; see Goffman, *Behavior,* p. 211.

26. See, for example: [Cook], *Coney Island,* p. 12; Slosson, "Amusement Business," p. 134; Robert Wilson Neal, "New York's City of Play," *World To-Day,* 11 (August 1906); 822; Elmer Blaney Harris, "The Day of Rest at Coney Island," *Everybody's Magazine,* 19 (July 1908): 24; Rollin Lynde Hartt, "The Amusement Park," *Atlantic Monthly,* 99 (May 1907): 668.

27. See Harvey Cox, *The Feast of Fools* (Cambridge, Mass.: Harvard University Press, 1969).

28. On the role of the grotesque in carnival, see Mikhail Bakhtin, *Rabelais and His World,* trans. Helene Iswalsky (Cambridge, Mass.: M.I.T. Press, 1968), esp. chap. 5.

29. McCullough, *Coney Island,* p. 255.

30. Reginald Wright Kauffman, "Why Is Coney?" *Hampton's Magazine,* 23 (August 1909): 224.

31. Edward F. Tilyou, "Human Nature with the Brakes Off—Or: Why the Schoolma'am Walked into the Sea," *American Magazine,* 94 (July 1922): 19, 21, 86, 92.

32. In my analysis of Coney Island's amusements I am indebted to Roger Caillois, *Man, Play, and Games,* trans. Meyer Barash (New York: Free Press, 1961).

33. *The New York Times,* 17 May 1903; Albert Bigelow Paine, "The New Coney Island," *Century,* 68 (August 1904): 535.

34. Thompson, "Amusing the Million," p. 385.

35. In my interpretation of the architecture of Luna Park, I have been stimulated by Robert Venturi, Denise Scott Brown, and Steven Izenour, *Learning from Las Vegas* (Cambridge, Mass.: M.I.T. Press, 1972); and also by Reyner Banham, *Los Angeles: The Architecture of Four Ecologies* (Middlesex, Eng.: Penguin Press, 1971), chap. 6.

36. Paine, "New Coney Island," 538.

37. Frederick [*sic*] A. Thompson, "The Summer Show," *Independent,* 62 (20 June 1907): 1460–61.

38. *The New York Times,* 17 May 1903 and 15 May 1904.

39. See Neil Harris, *Humbug: The Art of P. T. Barnum* (Boston: Little, Brown, 1973).

40. See Neil Harris, "The Culture of Catastrophe in Nineteenth-Century America" (Paper delivered at the University of North Carolina, Chapel Hill, 20 October 1975).

41. Kauffman, "Why Is Coney?" p. 217; on carnival laughter, see Bakhtin, *Rabelais,* pp. 11–12.

42. See Caillois, *Man, Play, and Games,* pp. 5–6.

43. Slosson, "Amusement Business," p. 136.

44. Thompson, "Amusing the Million," p. 386.

45. Paine, "New Coney Island," p. 537.

46. "The Mechanical Joys of Coney Island," *Scientific American,* 99 (15 August 1908): 109.

47. Thompson, "Amusing the Million," pp. 378–86.

48. *Seeing Coney Island of Today* (New York: Cupples & Leon, 1904), n.p.

49. *History of Coney Island: List and Photographs of Main Attractions* (New York: Burroughs and Company, 1904), p. 11.

50. On this subject, see Richard Cox, "Coney Island, Urban Symbol in American Art," New-York Historical Society *Quarterly,* 60 (January–April 1976): 35–52; and John I. H. Baur, *Revolution and Tradition in Modern American Art* (New York: Praeger, 1976), pp. 19–21.

51. Joseph Stella, "Discovery of America: Autobiographical Notes," *Art News,* 59 (November 1960): 64.

52. *Ibid.,* p. 65.

53. *Ibid.,* p. 65; Irma Jaffe, *Joseph Stella* (Cambridge, Mass.: Harvard University Press, 1970), pp. 40–42, 129–30.

54. Stella to Katherine Dreier, 26 September 1929, quoted in Jaffe, *Stella,* p. 58; Jaffe, *Stella,* pp. 129–30; Cox, "Coney Island," p. 41.

55. *John Sloan's New York Scene,* ed. Bruce St. John (New York: Harper & Row, 1965), pp. 140–41.

56. Edward Laning, *Sketchbooks of Reginald Marsh* (Greenwich, Conn.: New York Graphic Society, 1973), pp. 16, 22–24, 58; Lloyd Goodrich, *Reginald Marsh* (New York: Abrams, [1972]), p. 38.

57. Richard Le Gallienne, "Human Need of Coney Island," *Cosmopolitan,* 39 (July 1905): 243; Hartt, "Amusement Park," p. 670.

58. Slosson, "Amusement Business," p. 135.

59. Neal, "New York's City of Play," pp. 820–22.

60. James Huneker, *New Cosmopolis* (New York: Scribner's, 1915), p. 154.

61. *Ibid.,* pp. 154, 162, 164.

62. Edward Allsworth Ross, *Social Psychology* (New York: Macmillan, 1908), pp. 54–56, 46. See Nathan G. Hale, *Freud and the Americans: The Beginnings of Psychoanalysis in the United States, 1876–1917* (New York: Oxford University Press, 1971), p. 56; and Leo Bramson, *The Political Context of Sociology* (Princeton: Princeton University Press, 1961), chap. 3.

63. Huneker, *New Cosmopolis,* p. 158; Bruce Bliven, "Coney Island for Battered Souls," *New Republic,* 28 (23 November 1921): 374.

64. See Daniel M. Fox, "Introduction" to Simon N. Patten, *The New Basis of Civilization,* John Harvard Library (Cambridge, Mass.: Harvard University Press, 1968); and Fox, *The Discovery of Abundance: Simon N. Patten and the Transformation of Social Theory* (Ithaca: Cornell University Press, 1967).

65. Walter Rauschenbusch, *Christianizing the Social Order* (New York: Macmillan, 1912), pp. 248–49.

66. Jane Addams, *The Spirit of Youth and the City Streets* (New York: Macmillan, 1909), p. 69; Hartt, "Amusement Park," p. 677; see also Slosson, "Amusement Business," p. 135.

67. Richard Henry Edwards, *Popular Amusements* (New York: Association Press, 1915), p. 140; Edwards, *Christianity and Amusements* (New York: Association Press, 1915), pp. 16, 99–100.

68. On cultural authority and the movies, see Robert Sklar, *Movie-Made America* (New York: Random House, 1975), pp. 18–19.

69. Luther H. Gulick, "Play in Democracy," quoted in Clarence E. Rainwater, *The Play Movement in the United States* (Chicago: University of Chicago Press, 1922), p. 278. In addition to Rainwater, see Lawrence A. Finfer, "Leisure as Social Work in the Urban Community: The Progressive Recreation Movement, 1890–1912" (Ph.D. diss., Michigan State University, 1974), esp. pp. 163–91; and Dominick Joseph Cavallo, "The Child in American Reform: A Psychohistory of the Movement to Organize Children's Play, 1880–1920" (Ph.D. diss., State University of New York at Stony Brook, 1976).

70. Quoted in George Elliott Howard, "Social Psychology of the Spectator," *American Journal of Sociology*, 18 (July 1912): 41.

71. Patten, *New Basis of Civilization*, pp. 128–29, 136–37, 125, 131–32.

72. On this change and its ramifications, see Robert Sklar, "Introduction," *The Plastic Age, 1917–1930* (New York: Braziller, 1970), pp. 3, 16–19; Otis Pease, *The Responsibilities of American Advertising* (New Haven: Yale University Press, 1958), chap. 2; Stuart Ewen, *Captains of Consciousness: Advertising and the Social Roots of the Consumer Culture* (New York: McGraw-Hill, 1976); and Christopher Lasch, "The Narcissistic Personality of Our Time," *Partisan Review*, 44 (1977): 9–19.

73. On the interlocking character of amusement and work, see Max Horkheimer and Theodor W. Adorno, "The Culture Industry: Enlightenment as Mass Deception," in *Dialectic of Enlightenment*, trans. John Cumming (New York: Herder and Herder, 1972), esp. p. 137.

74. Maxim Gorky, "Boredom," *Independent*, 63 (8 August 1907): 311–12, 313–14.

75. *Ibid.*, p. 309.

76. For various views of the function of carnival and its relation to the social order, see Caillois, *Man, Play, and Games*; Keith Thomas, "Work and Leisure in Pre-Industrial Society," *Past and Present*, 29 (December 1964): 53–54; Turner, *Ritual Process*, chaps. 3–5; Bakhtin, *Rabelais*, chaps. 1–2; and Natalie Zemon Davis, *Society and Culture in Early Modern France* (Stanford: Stanford University Press, 1975), chap. 4. See also Herbert Marcuse, "On Hedonism," in *Negations: Essays in Critical Theory*, trans. Jeremy J. Shapiro (Boston: Beacon Press, 1968), pp. 159–200.

77. Kauffman, "Why Is Coney?" p. 224.

78. George F. Dobson, quoted in Pilat and Ranson, *Sodom*, p. 172.

79. McCullough, *Coney Island*, p. 316.

80. The other singly owned amusement park currently at Coney Island is Astroland.

81. Tilyou, "Human Nature," p. 91.

82. Dr. Martin Arthur Couney, quoted in Pilat and Ranson, *Sodom*, p. 199.

ILLUSTRATION CREDITS